KATHRYN M. IRELAND
A LIFE IN DESIGN

CELEBRATING 30 YEARS OF INTERIORS

CICO BOOKS

LONDON NEW YORK

To Georgina Alice, our latest addition to the family

Creative Director: Leslie Harrington
Senior Commissioning Editor:
  Annabel Morgan
Head of Production: Patricia Harrington
Index: Hilary Bird

First published in the United Kingdom
in 2023 by CICO Books
An imprint of Ryland Peters & Small Ltd
20–21 Jockey's Fields
London WC1R 4BW
and
341 E 116th Street
New York, NY 10029
www.rylandpeters.com

For photography credits, see pages 268.
Every reasonable effort has been made
to identify the copyright holders of
photographs featured in this book. If any
have been inadvertently overlooked, the
publisher would be glad to hear from them
and to include any necessary credits in any
subsequent reprint or edition.

ISBN: 978-1-80065-277-4

Printed and bound in China.
10 9 8 7 6 5 4 3 2 1

A CIP catalog record for this book is avilable
from the Library of Congress and the
British Library.

MIX
Paper from
responsible sources
FSC® C106563

CONTENTS

INTRODUCTION

A *Life in Design* is a recollection of residential design projects that have been, in various ways, significant to me over the course of my thirty years as an interior designer. Throughout the book, you will be presented with twenty of my greatest homes, traveling from the West Coast to the East, with the finale in Europe. As a lifelong movie buff, I have paired each project with the name of one of my favorite films.

The world of interior design wasn't on my radar when I left London as an ambitious twenty-something bound for Los Angeles in the late 1980s. From a young age, apart from horses, houses interested me the most, and quickly turned into my profession and passion. It all began in a Santa Monica garage, and that is pretty much where I've ended up, although my current hub of operations is much grander. I always say I have three offices—Los Angeles, London, and my Mini. It isn't necessary to staff a huge office if you've got a wonderful crew. My mantra is to hire the best people, respect them, and reward them. Ultimately, it's all about chemistry.

I am completely self-taught, a true autodidact in the world of aesthetics, design, renovation, and architecture. Being British, I've lived among antiques and vintage my whole life and see value in preservation. My mother Lillian, with a knack for interior design and an inclination to live stylishly, raised me and my siblings between London and Scotland with holidays spent in a Palladian villa in the Veneto, a stately home in the north of England, or our fisherman's cottage on the west coast of Scotland. Those houses taught me a fundamental understanding of proportion and symmetry and balance with which to adhere or depart.

At the heart of my process are my relationships with my clients. There is always a sense of intimacy and satisfaction in helping families realize and create homes in which to live their lives and, as a result of the protracted interior design process, many clients have become dear friends and members of my extended family. Speaking of family, I've been very fortunate to have my brother Robert on board to manage construction projects with me, while my sister Mary Jane, a highly esteemed interior designer in Ireland, has been a constant source of support and creative inspiration. My son Otis has followed in my footsteps in the textiles business with a successful line of his own, Otis Textiles. Throughout the book, you will see six of my own homes at various points in my life. Very often, our best work is that which we do for ourselves. But even the homes that belong to my clients are houses I could picture myself living in. I hope you enjoy this glimpse into my work and my world, and that it brings inspiration to your own home.

How It All Began

Four months after moving to Los Angeles, I met the most handsome man ever. He turned out to be a filmmaker for the original *Saturday Night Live* team. We met, married and had three boys within four years. I only bothered to ask him what he did when an invitation for the Grammys arrived, and it turned out that he was a nominee. Anyway, that story will be in my memoirs, but this is a decorating book.

Once I became a mother, the early starts demanded by my music video career were no longer on the cards. My actress friend Amanda Pays and I turned my husband's editing studio on Santa Monica's main street into a shop selling decorative accessories. We were both becoming homemakers and, tired of not finding things for the house, we decided to bring back unique items from our trips back home. Ireland Pays became an overnight success, thanks to *House & Garden* US, who featured a full-page photo of Amanda and me, taken by Dewey Nicks, that kickstarted our retail business. The shop was a landmark—not much bigger than a cupboard, but stuffed full of antique fabrics and bits and pieces that make a home. We soon had a cult following.

In one of my past lives, I had written for *Ritz* magazine, the UK version of Andy Warhol's *Interview*, and, as luck would have it, Nancy Novograd, the editor-in-chief of *House & Garden* US at the time, asked me to write an article on Amanda Pays and Corbin Bernson's recently renovated home for the magazine (commissioned by Wendy Goodman as sitting editor, and with Oberto Gili as photographer). In this way, I was catapulted into the higher echelons of editorial, and over the course of my career have continued to write and been a contributing editor for many magazines, including *Domino*, *Elle Decor*, and *House Beautiful*, as well as writing six books on interior design.

That article proved to be pivotal in more ways than one. When our friend Steve Martin mentioned he was searching for a new home, one that looked and felt exactly like mine, Amanda's overgrown cottage leapt to mind. I took Steve to look round and he immediately saw that this could be his home. With me as his guide, we set about turning playrooms into billiard rooms, hanging curtains, and amassing art and antiques to fill the walls. This was my very first professional job as an interior designer.

ABOVE Nico, the then Marchioness of Londonderry, my mother, and Lady Annabel Goldsmith were my design inspirations. Nico had the best taste of anyone. She renovated her family's stately home in the north of England at the age of 18 with the help of David Hicks, who showed so many of us the way.

OPPOSITE My first venture in interior design was when I turned Gary's and my editing suite into a pillow shop. Amanda Pays and I arrived in Los Angeles at the same time and both of us were newlyweds and wanting to make homes. This *House & Garden* photo from 1990 threw us into the public eye. With the launch of my first fabric collection and Amanda moving back to England, I moved on to Santa Monica and opened a larger shop to sell my wares. My French farmhouse is a source of inspiration to this day. Quilt in Red was my first print and colorway and it still sells 25 years later.

Movie producer
Kathryn Ireland (*far left*), who with television actress Amanda Pays (*left*) opened a decorative accessories shop in Santa Monica last spring, says, "As transplanted Brits, we discovered it was hard to find nicely designed finishing touches in L.A." Time between takes is limited for both women, but, says Ireland, "Whenever we go to England, we find ourselves lugging back more linen and lamps." (Ireland Pays, 2428 Main St., Santa Monica, CA; 213-396-3035).

The Design Process

Every client and every house is unique, and as my job brings about such a personal relationship with both, I now find myself interviewing prospective clients just as much as they are interviewing me. Ideally, I like to meet potential clients, visit their project or, if it's a build from the ground up, invite them to my own house to show them how I live.

In the early days of my career, one relied upon editorial coverage and word of mouth for work. Today the client tends to be more educated and will have done much research on which designer to use and the style they want. Online courses such as Create Academy and design retreats like the ones I started at my home in France and by taking groups to the Cotswolds and Marrakech have become invaluable tools for both homemakers and for up-and-coming designers. I'm a big believer in setting a budget then under-promising and over-delivering by coming in on time and on budget. Being realistic is the key to success, and having happy clients that continue to ask you to work with them is the ultimate accolade.

Once the involvement of my role is clear (I enjoy a collaboration, but am also happy either being given a brief or simply being left to my own devices), the contract has been drawn up, and the budget agreed, then I go to work on the design presentation. First-time clients working with interior designers have to be educated about fees, markups, and costs. Michael S. Smith once gave me some great advice: "You never want to be anyone's first-time decorator." Thank you, Michael.

The next step is putting together the presentation—lots of sketches and mood boards that show how the finished house will look, with all the details of paint colours, fabrics, surfaces, flooring, and so on. Fabric is my passion, so that's usually where I start a scheme. Alternatively, there might be a particular piece of art or furniture or another object that the client wants to retain, in which case I will need to know about that from the start.

Like filmmaking, there are so many trades involved in a successful design project. Over the years I have worked with many of the great architects and landscapers and a handful of designers are my close friends. We have all worked together, advice being given when needed. We all share sources and, on occasion, clients.

Technology has changed the way we work. Some years ago, I founded an online website called The Perfect Room. One could shop an array of designers' rooms with the collaboration of the designer and make selections that would fit a budget. Today, with offices shrinking, clients no longer demand as many face-to-face meetings and the mood boards and meetings have all gone online, while Google Docs makes

staying in touch with clients and vendors so much easier. Virtual communications make decisions instantaneous and keep projects moving along swiftly. However, there's nothing to replace the feeling of being face to face with your team and seeing spaces as they develop.

LEFT AND ABOVE With both new builds and renovations, the key to a successful room is in the presentation. A drawing or sketch of what the room will look like, including a floor plan, is invaluable. Selecting the fabrics and furnishings is just as important, the more organized the better. Although for me the process can change as my ideas evolve, once the fabrics are chosen they are locked in. Much of the furniture I use is antique, but some pieces are custom made in my atelier; this comes later on.

The Fabrics

Each designer will have their own starting point for a design scheme, and for me it's fabric and color— I love the transformative effect they can have on any interior.

I've been interested in textiles from an early age, but it wasn't until a visit to West Africa in my early twenties that I began collecting. The rare vintage pieces and random scraps picked up on my travels, along with this enduring passion of mine, provided the foundation for my own fabric collections, which are featured at intervals throughout this book.

I design as an interior designer rather than a textile designer, so come at the process from a different angle—it's a bit like painting by numbers. Every room scheme needs three or four fabrics, so for my first collection, Quilt, I created six designs in six different colorways, all of which could be mixed and matched and were guaranteed to work perfectly together. Subsequent collections came about whenever I felt that there was a gap that needed to be filled—after Quilt, for example, came Toile, as I wanted a check and a stripe to work alongside the paisleys and florals of my first collection. Since then, I've added versatile weaves and sheers plus patterns to suit many styles, seasons, and different interiors.

During a break from living in London, my middle son Otis was helping me out by taking a look at the finances of the fabric business. I was completely taken aback when he announced that he would be interested in joining the business, but as he would be giving

up his formative years he wanted to partner with me. It didn't take him very long to figure out which way the warp or the weft ran or the advantages of hand-printing versus digital. He made many connections and after a visit to the Como Textile Fair was confident enough to launch his own company, Otis Textiles, a line of luxurious plains (mohairs, corduroys, cashmeres and linens) which, funnily enough, work well with my designs.

Unlike fashion, fabric designs have long lives—my first and second collections still sell as well today as they did when first launched. I've added wallpapers and continue to grow the line with new ideas, but every now and then I recolor the original designs. When I opened my own print shop in Los Angeles, the idea was to offer designers custom colorways and have virtually everything in stock.

When putting this book together, it was hard to decide which houses to include. I decided to focus on residential projects and to structure the book geographically, from the West to East coast of the US then over to Europe. The obvious way to go may be chronologically, but I felt this way would tell my bi-coastal, bi-continental story better.

ABOVE LEFT My third collection was inspired by a trip to Bali and I continued to add to the color palette and designs that were already in the line. At the time, these colors and prints were unique and fresh. I have continued to use this as my trademark.

ABOVE AND RIGHT With hand printing being taken over by digital methods, and textile designing becoming more prominent, I decided to open my own print shop. At first I planned to use it just for samples and color, but when I saw the opportunity to buy an 8,000-square-foot building, I realized I would be able to print most of my line. The silk screens and pots of paint, seen above, are such a visual feast; it's like going to playschool every day. Printing by hand is such a skilled art. As with dancing, it is very important to be in sync with your partner at all times. Making sure the screens match up is key, otherwise you are left with yards of unsellable fabric.

BATIK

After a trip to Indonesia, I was seduced by Balinese batiks and collected a series of 19th-century designs that inspired this collection. Based on tradition, what makes my collection stand out from others is the sense of color and scale.

AS GOOD AS IT GETS

My current home on the flats of Santa Monica is very close to where my family lived for over 20 years. My three boys, Oscar, Otis, and Louis, were able to skateboard to school, only getting in the car to go to the beach. Although this property doesn't hold the same memories as their childhood home, it has very much the same sort of feeling. The pieces I brought with me—art, furniture, and rugs—give the place the sense of our previous home, but it has the advantages of up-to-date plumbing, an abundance of light, and a floorplan that our Spanish Revival farmhouse couldn't achieve without adding a wing.

When I downsized from our original family home, I was able to open a print studio and start printing. Every decorator now thought they could become a textile designer, and the few hand-print shops operating in Europe and the US were overwhelmed. Lead times had become prohibitive, and I realized that printing my own fabrics would keep showrooms happy and timings on track.

All three of my boys had moved to New York, and I was up for a project. One day, my son Otis called me. He had got his real estate license and was scouring LA for properties of interest. He spotted a project for me on the Santa Monica flats, situated on a street that was still up-and-coming. It was a Spanish-style bungalow with an interesting history. In the 1970s, the previous owners had obtained permission to build a studio in the garden. In the early '90s, their son inherited the property and hired Mexican architect Ruben Ojeda to enlarge the original house.

On my first visit, I walked into what appeared to be a little cottage then through into what could be a small addition to London's Tate Gallery, with west-facing windows and soaring ceilings. Through the French doors was a yard that I could see in my mind's eye as the courtyard of a Moroccan riad. A detached garage had been semi-converted into a home gym and could be redesigned to make a guest cottage. But what really sealed the deal was the modern two-story structure at the back of the plot. This space, with its polished concrete floors, sliding wooden doors, and vast windows, would make an extraordinary home office. It was love at first sight,

PAGE 18 The yard that connected the house to the garage and studio was a challenge, with little to work with, apart from a single cactus. This inspired me to create a riad-style courtyard with drought-tolerant landscaping.

PAGES 20-21 In the sitting room, garage-style double doors from Chateau Domingue and an early 19th-century suzani are the stars of the show. A Balinese daybed from Waldo's Designs many years ago, seen here as a coffee table with a selection of favorite objects, has been used in every one of my homes. The chairs are from my Pied à Terre collection, the simple rug from Amadi Carpets, and the side tables from Arteriors.

RIGHT Another pair of custom doors from Chateau Domingue bookends the property in my studio, which also serves as an entertaining space. The curtain fabric is my Safi Suzani in Chocolate Cherry.

OPPOSITE For several years I was the muse and spokesperson for AGA in North America, so cooking on any other stove was a no-no. Floor-to-ceiling shelving houses my party pieces, from candles to plates.

and I jumped through every hoop to acquire what would become my new home.

Renovations started, and I became project manager, architect, and landscaper—having over-spent to acquire the property, I had to wear a lot of hats. But the fun of doing this house was that I could renovate it in one fell swoop and bring my vision to life. Having three boys (and six of their friends over on any given afternoon), one thing I was determined to have was a generously sized kitchen and family room where eight large men could sprawl on the sofa watching the ball game while I cooked supper on my ever-loyal AGA. In fact, this house, with its two bedrooms, has ended up with two kitchens.

RIGHT I'd really wanted a house with ocean views, so the Stephen Wilkes photograph of Santa Monica Pier from Peter Fetterman Gallery is the focal point of this room. The sofa and ottoman, both custom-made by my own studio, and the throw pillows are all covered in Otis Textiles' Georgina linen in various colors, while the chair in the foreground is also Otis Textiles. I brought back the leather pouffes from a trip to Morocco and the wall light is from Obsolete in Los Angeles.

LEFT AND OPPOSITE The two bedrooms and dressing room upstairs were reorganized to make a larger main bedroom suite. In the dressing room, the wallpaper and matching curtain are in my Greta Reverse Taupe (left). The Italian marquetry commode came from my grandfather's house in Alexandria, Egypt—he went there to seek his fortune in this late teens—and the mirror from Julian Chichester. An Indian embroidery from Ahmedabad covers the bed. My old faithful Chesterfield sofa has been reupholstered many times over the years and is seen here in Bouquet Aubergine from my British Isles collection (opposite).

LEFT A custom-made chair and ottoman in Lilac Red from my Sur La Plage collection in the reading nook that leads into my bedroom.

BELOW AND OPPOSITE This is a more modern bathroom than I'm used to, with Caesarstone quartz covering the walls and floor. The vanity and mirror are by Fantini Plumbing from Snyder Diamond in Santa Monica. The floral painting is by French artist Jean Verrechia, who lives and works on St. Barths in the Caribbean.

The finished house draws together all the separate strands of my life: family, creativity, travel, and motherhood.

OPPOSITE This four-poster bed of my design has traveled from the guest house of our very first family home on 18th Street in Santa Monica to Louis' bedroom in this house. The bedcover fabric is my Kirkbean design, while the drapes are an Otis Textiles sheer. A painting by my childhood friend India Jane Birley hangs on the wall.

RIGHT My love of wallpaper re-emerged while decorating this house. For this bathroom, I chose Quilt Reverse in Blue and Silver Metallic. A simple Italian trestle table with a marble basin is teamed with a mirror from Arteriors. The light fixture from Circa Lighting was originally used in my shop in Almont Yard, West Hollywood—I love to recycle. The Ashes and Snow picture, which sits above an African chair, was a present from the artist, Gregory Colbert.

OPPOSITE This outdoor space, under an overhang that was a useless part of the house, is now a favorite eating area. I built the seating on either side of the kitchen door for alfresco dining.

ABOVE My son Otis inherited my love of houses. Having got his real estate license, he found this property and knew at once that it was what I was looking for. It was dated, with far too many built-ins for me, but it had the square footage and some wonderful features for indoor/outdoor living.

LEFT At the entrance to the house, through a wooden door, I installed a firepit in front of the sliding doors into the living room. This is the fireplace the house was missing.

The deciding factor for buying the property was this two-story building designed by Koning Eizenberg Architecture in the late 20th century. Its founders Hank Koning and Julie Eizenberg are contemporaries of Frank Gehry and are considered important Los Angeles architects. The Willy Guhl planters and chairs are from Inner Gardens in Culver City.

THE SECRET GARDEN

andscape designer Stephen Block and I met at a *House Beautiful* magazine showcase home many years ago in Los Angeles. Not only did we make an immediate connection, but we soon discovered that our design processes are remarkably similar—both of us have a definite idea of the effect we wish to achieve, but are willing to embrace the magic of improvisation.

Stephen and I work instinctively rather than formally, moving elements into and out of spaces, over-acquiring materials and editing on site. We both like to get our hands dirty—I'm a girl who hangs my own curtains and sews the hems, while Stephen loves to roll up his sleeves and get planting. So, when it was time for Gary and I to upgrade our backyard in Santa Monica, Stephen immediately came to mind. We wanted to build a pool to make the most of the glorious Southern California climate and with Stephen's help I drew up plans for a lush, palm-filled space that brought my vision of an untamed, abundantly planted Spanish finca garden to life.

Naturally, I was delighted to return the favor when Stephen and his costume designer wife Julie asked me to help redecorate the interiors of their Spanish Colonial Revival home. They had just wrapped up work with an architect on structural updates to the house that preserved its period floor plan and early Californian architectural detailing. For the final stage of their 21st-century facelift, the couple wanted to infuse the historic home with new life, and my brief was a top-to-bottom interior revamp, including the bedrooms of their three adorable daughters.

Stephen and Julie's house was very much a family home—in fact, it reminded me of my own, filled with children and barking dogs—nothing was too precious. The couple already had plenty of existing furnishings, art, and accessories for me to work with, but the 'zhuzh' also gave me the perfect opportunity to incorporate our mutual love of color and textiles into their home.

The many windows, French doors, outdoor balconies, and patios of this house all lead out into Stephen's glorious gardens, which were designed as a series of outdoor rooms perfect for both family life and grown-up entertaining. As is my style, I kept the window treatments simple.

PAGE 36 The South Garden is full of luxuriant staghorn ferns, camellias, and agaves, planted in gravel for an elegant European feel.

ABOVE The entrance hall has retained its original Spanish Colonial features that date to the 1920s. The Spanish table is from Stephen's company Inner Gardens.

RIGHT In the dining room, the table came from a buying trip to France. The chair fabric is Bennison, while curtains in my Safi Suzani print flank the fireplace.

PAGES 40–41 In the family room, a mishmash of my patterns and weaves covers the sofas and window seat. The curtains are Quilt in Yellow from my first collection. The Minotti sofa and Eames chair and ottoman are all upholstered in Otis Textiles, while the coffee table is from my Pied à Terre collection designed for Grange.

LEFT The sofa is upholstered in Otis Textiles with various pillows covered in my fabrics. The vintage rug was sourced at Amadi Carpets. The shelves hold treasured objects collected by Stephen and Julie over the years.

ABOVE The unusual 1920s cast-iron table came from Inner Gardens and is home to a Song dynasty jar, an Indonesian mask, and an Anduze vase. The painting above is by Corey Daniels.

Roman shades and curtains hang from
hand-forged iron rings and rods, and when it
came to the furnishings, I mixed and matched
Stephen and Julie's favorite items with newly
upholstered pieces using fabric from several
of my collections, including my latest release
at the time, the vibrant Mexico Meets
Morocco line. Everywhere, I introduced rich
hues, bold prints, and hand-blocked patterns
that worked beautifully with the creamy walls
and the vivid, jewel-like greens of the gardens.

Together with the architect, we created
a charming and comfortable home, at once
respectful of its historic Spanish Colonial
heritage yet infused with the vitality and
spirit of this exuberant, artistic family.

THIS PAGE AND OPPOSITE The focal point of the master bedroom is a custom-made bed from Indigo Seas. Stephen found the painting of Provence on his travels. All the fabrics are my own, except the antique Indian textile that I repurposed for a bed bolster.

OPPOSITE AND RIGHT The Block girls handpicked the fabrics and colors for their bedrooms, two of which are shown here. The bed curtains were handwoven in Marrakech (opposite), while the other fabrics are a mixture of my Mexico Meets Morocco and Batik collections. Artworks and special treasures are displayed throughout.

OPPOSITE The patio off the kitchen has a metal and polished concrete table from Stephen's Inner Gardens collection paired with a set of vintage wood and metal chairs.

BELOW En route to the front door is a Texas shell-stone-topped table that's home to a garland of cast-iron roses and other assorted garden antiques. The decorative wall light above is original to the house.

RIGHT AND BELOW RIGHT The various pots, vases, antique garden ornaments, and plants were all sourced from Inner Gardens.

QUILT

My very first fabric collection, Quilt, was launched in 1997 and was inspired by a late 18th-century patchwork quilt. The six patterns and colorways have proven to be the foundation for all my fabric collections to come.

LA STORY

I t was while my ex-husband Gary and I were on our honeymoon at legendary producer Lorne Michaels' home in Amagansett that I first met Steve Martin and Victoria Tennant, who between them were to kick-start my career as an interior designer. Steve and Gary had been friends and collaborators during the early days of *Saturday Night Live*, for which Gary directed dozens of comedic shorts, and Steve was, well, Steve Martin.

Not long after the birth of my third son Louis, Steve came to dinner at our house in Santa Monica (see pages 76–87) with news that he was selling his modernist Beverly Hills home with its amazing collection of contemporary art (Steve has become as well-known for his art collection as his comedy). Although our lives could not have been more different—I was up to my ears in barking dogs, attention-seeking children, and a busy husband—Steve mentioned that he'd love a house like my own. Post-divorce, he wanted a smaller home, charming and comfortable—something, he said, exactly like ours.

I had just written a piece for *House & Garden* detailing the renovation of a Beverly Hills home by my friend and business partner Amanda Pays and her actor husband Corbin Bernsen. While house hunting, Amanda and Corbin had stumbled upon a nondescript cottage and fallen in love with its large and well-situated hillside lot. To accommodate their family, they expanded the house using reclaimed materials to create a rambling farmhouse complete with beamed ceilings, a spacious kitchen, and plenty of bedrooms. However, after the refurbishment, Amanda's homesickness for England took hold, and the whole gang packed up and headed for the English countryside.

PAGES 52–53 The pair of French chairs was found locally and the Northern European mirror over the fireplace came from Lief in Los Angeles. The Kashmiri side table was from my first store, Ireland Pays.

LEFT In the sitting room, the curtains are crewelwork from Chelsea Textiles. The various pillows came from Ireland Pays and the coffee table from Lief.

I took Steve to see it the next day and, as I had suspected, the house and garden immediately captured his imagination. It was the right place for him, but he needed a decorator to create a house that looked and felt like mine. And that is how I fell into my first professional job as an interior designer.

To start, the two of us reviewed the paintings Steve thought would work—mostly landscapes, both Californian and European. I put to one side the vivid colors and prints that I usually gravitate toward, instead picking out fabrics in subtle tones and interesting textures. I designed simple yet luxurious curtains to hang at the abundance of windows and French doors, and arranged the reception rooms into relaxed seating areas, conducive to conversation or an impromptu banjo session. Sofas and armchairs were upholstered in sea foam and cream shades, providing a restful backdrop for pillows in leafy florals that echoed the gardens surrounding the property.

Steve wanted a place that was consistent with his personality: quiet, relaxed, and a lot of fun. This was exactly where we ended up. I created a hideaway, a sanctuary, a pleasing home in which he still lives today. Later, I would work with Steve on his New York apartment and a Santa Barbara retreat, but this first collaboration remains my favorite.

"With Kathryn, you can shut your eyes, open them five months later, and everything will be perfect."—Steve Martin

LEFT I found the four early Italian chairs on the East Coast. Over the fireplace hangs a landscape by Californian artist Terry Delapp. The huge carpet was sourced at J.H. Minassian, Los Angeles.

ABOVE AND OPPOSITE In the main bedroom, the four-poster was custom-designed by KMI Studio, Santa Monica. I found the late 18th-century circular Irish mirror and the 18th-century Swedish desk from Lief, Los Angeles. The runner carpet, also from J.H. Minassian, leads the eye to another Terry Delapp painting at the end of the hallway.

WEST SIDE STORY

ometimes the nature of a creative collaboration with a client spawns rich synergies with other design professionals, and every so often I find myself astonished by the degree to which a completed project can exceed the sum of its parts. This is how I would describe my most recent work with my client, noted jewelry designer Nancy Newberg, on the Westside, Los Angeles home she shares with her husband Bruce. The finished house is a luxurious contemporary reinterpretation of the Spanish Colonial Revival style that both Nancy and I adore.

I've known the Newbergs for many years. We both have three sons of similar ages, and thanks to our children, who attended the same preschool, we have many friends in common. I worked on the couple's previous house in LA, coming in at the end of the project once the house was built and helping Nancy over the years as her boys grew. It is always fun and inspiring to work with someone who has similar expertise and appreciation.

For many years, Nancy, her husband, and their sons had lived nearby, in a house layered with European antiques, majolica, textiles, and color, all of which worked beautifully for that house at that period of Nancy's life. But now her sons had grown and flown the nest, and she was more than ready for a change of pace and a new challenge.

For one of Nancy's birthdays, she wanted to go and visit Belgian designer Axel Vervoordt's chateau and workshops in Antwerp. Knowing Axel, I was able to arrange this for her. Axel's style—unfussy, uncomplicated, and uncluttered without being bland, severe, or harsh—captivated Nancy, who was beguiled by the luxurious yet almost monastic simplicity of his interiors. It was there that she had a cathartic moment—out with the old and in with the new. She thought that she wanted not only to downsize the square footage of her house but also to declutter and pare down the contents.

Not long after this, when a fabulous piece of property that Nancy had long admired came on the market on the next-door street, I was delighted that she wanted to include me in the

PAGES 60 AND 61 In the library, the Minotti chairs are upholstered in emerald green Rogers & Goffigon mohair, while the dining table with inlaid brass accents is by KMI Studio (page 60). The planters flanking the front door are by Willy Guhl from Inner Gardens (page 61).

THIS PAGE The floors throughout the house are by Exquisite Surfaces Beverly Hills and the light fixtures are KMI Studio. The table is from Obsolete in Culver City, while the mirror glimpsed to the right is one of a few pieces from the Blanchard Collective in Marlborough, England. The artworks are by Olafur Eliasson.

monumental task of building on this stunning lot overlooking the ocean. The existing Tudor-style house standing on the plot bore no resemblance to the Wallace Neff- or Roland Coate-style house that Nancy envisaged sitting in its place. In fact, the only thing that was to survive from the original house were the chimney stacks.

Once the purchase was secured, the next step was to find the right architect for the job. We had interviewed all the usual suspects when Nancy went out on a limb and suggested Marmol Radziner, who are best known for clean-lined contemporary houses that feature huge expanses of glass. She asked them to depart from their usual style and design a new house for her and Bruce, one that merged the romance of the Spanish style with the simplified and sleek aesthetic of 21st-century modernism.

The result is a house with a horseshoe-shaped floor plan encircling a new pool and gardens designed by Stephen Block. The steel-framed arched windows and French doors allow natural light to pour in and recreate Axel's minimalist aesthetic of uncluttered spaces and unadorned walls, which had inspired this departure. The subtle yet monumental architectural detailing and creative lighting design provide a sense of warmth, history, and intimacy that so many new-build homes lack.

While architect Ron Radziner and Stephen got to grips with the whole deconstruction and reconstruction process, Nancy and I were adopting a new approach to the interiors. We traveled to Europe to source pieces from both Parma and Paris for

OPPOSITE The loggia is a much lived-in space. I found the light fixture at Nickey Kehoe and the sofas were made by KMI Studio and upholstered in Georgina in Oatmeal by Otis Textiles. The leather chair came from JF Chen, Los Angeles, and the coffee table from Italy.

RIGHT In the cloakroom, the custom sink and vanity is by Marmol Radziner, and the elegant hanging lights are from Alison Berger Glassworks.

the house. To meet the terms of my brief and fill the spacious rooms of the new house, I had many pieces of furniture custom-made in my studio, including the lighting. Paint was used judiciously and to excellent effect, and while I didn't completely avoid my signature layering of fabrics, I kept mostly to neutral tones and pared-back window treatments. Luckily, my son Otis had just launched Otis Textiles, his line of woven plains, which were all being made in Italy, Belgium, and France, and were perfect for these simple yet luxurious interiors.

Ron's architecture, my furnishings, and Stephen's planting all came together to create a harmonious whole. I have to confess that at first I was a little dubious about working with an architect who is more at home designing

OPPOSITE The walls throughout the house have an acrylic plaster finish rather than the traditional kind—Ron's choice, as it provides an attractive texture and prevents cracking. The upstairs hallway is home to a rustic table.

ABOVE The sofas were custom made for this space by KMI Studio and dressed with an assortment of hand-dyed velvet pillows from Kirsten Hecktermann. Over the fireplace hangs a ceramic artwork by Italian ceramicist Bruno Gambone. The custom-made coffee table was inspired by one that Nancy and I spotted at the Luis Laplace atelier in Paris, and the unusual Swedish standing lamp was sourced at Galerie Half in Los Angeles.

with glass, but the end results completely belied my doubts. Nancy had the foresight to realize that we were, in fact, a perfect team for this project.

The Newbergs' new house looks and feels as if it has always occupied the site, and George Washington Smith, Roland Coate, or Wallace Neff, the great masters of the California style, would no doubt salute Nancy's choices—she has created a Spanish Revival home perfect for today's way of living.

LEFT The kitchen is simple and sophisticated. The ceiling lights are the Boccia pendant by Luigi Caccia Dominioni for Azucena, found on a buying trip in Paris with Nancy. Marmol Raziner designed and built the island.

ABOVE In the sunny breakfast room, a marble-topped Saarinen Tulip table is teamed with chairs found at Nickey Kehoe. Sheer curtains hang from iron rods.

In the formal dining room, the light fixtures above the table are from Alison Berger Glassworks for Holly Hunt. The dining table, custom-made by KMI Studio, can comfortably seat 12. The dining chairs, complete with their original leather, are by Jacob Kjaer.

ABOVE AND LEFT The main bathroom has a freestanding Waterworks bathtub and faucets from the Henry collection. In the dressing room, the cabinets were designed by Marmol Raziner, with custom hardware and a three-way mirror from KMI Studio. The 1970s Danish chaise was found at Therien & Co., Los Angeles.

OPPOSITE The custom wrought-iron bed was designed and made by KMI Studio. The fabric on the sofa and curtains is Otis Textiles, and the bedside tables are from Charles Jacobsen, Los Angeles.

ABOVE A mixture of custom and RH outdoor furniture is grouped under the overhang of the guest house. All the outdoor lighting was custom designed by KMI Studio.

OPPOSITE ABOVE In the sitting area of the guest house, a sofa and coffee table from Nickey Kehoe are teamed with KMI Studio chairs covered in vintage indigo throws. The blue rug is by Christopher Farr.

OPPOSITE BELOW In the guest house bedroom, the custom bed and bedside tables are by KMI Studio, while the rug is from Vandra Rugs. The custom cashmere blanket on the bed is from Otis Textiles and the retro bench and chair were found at JF Chen, Los Angeles.

The house's serene, monastic mood was inspired by Nancy's visit to Axel Vervoordt's Kanaal project in Antwerp.

THE PARENT TRAP

For the first few years of married life, Gary and I lived all over the Westside of Los Angeles, in a series of rentals, from a shack at the beach to a house with a ballroom. But with two small boys and a third on the way, the time had come to abandon our vagabond ways and buy a house large enough for our growing family. We wanted to live in that part of LA that presses up against the Santa Monica mountains and catches sea breezes from the nearby Pacific. So, on days off from the high-octane energy that defines music video production, I toured and curb-stalked and made offers on many houses in Santa Monica north of Montana, as it's known today. But I was always outbid. Very, very annoying. The leisurely process of buying a French house (see page 252) had in no way prepared me for the onslaught of other equally eager buyers.

One day, I dragged myself to a newly listed property—what looked to me like a rustic farmhouse set in the foothills of southern Spain. It was, in fact, a four-bedroom Spanish Colonial Revival-style property, north of Montana Avenue and totally out of our price range. Built in 1923, the house was slightly run-down, but brimmed with architectural authenticity. Inside, the character-defining features of early 20th-century California style—arched doorways, original fireplaces, vaulted ceilings, and a living room with a large bay window—enticed me with thrilling design possibilities. I completely fell for the house. However, inventory is limited for pre-war homes in this area, and Santa Monica is a perennial seller's market. So when our offer wasn't accepted, I decamped to France, where the boys spent the summer term in the village school. Months later, on our return to Santa Monica, my real estate agent called with the news that the owner was now eager to sell. Suddenly and unexpectedly, this out-of-reach lost cause was ours to use as a springboard for a new phase of family life.

We moved in as soon as we were able with our young sons and a jumble of possessions and pets. Buying the house had nearly cleaned us out, and all we could afford in the way of decorating was a fresh coat of paint. I furnished the house with items I'd found at garage sales, flea-market curtains, and my first costly investment of an English Chesterfield sofa covered in Rose Cumming fabrics, plus two chairs from Indigo Seas. This immediately gave the house that sense that we'd lived there for decades, which is now, of course, my signature style. With a friendly and relaxed yet intimate mood, the interiors fused my love for classic English country style with a youthful and laid-back Californian spirit.

Our home in Santa Monica was where I further developed my love for beautiful fabrics and antique textiles, and worked out how to hand-tie and properly spring a sofa *à la style Anglaise*.

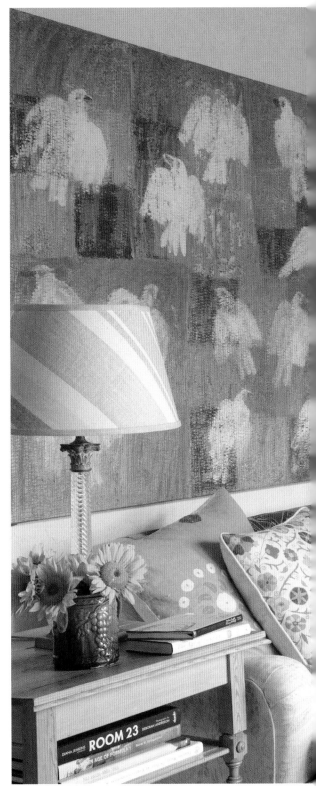

PAGE 76 Once the trampoline was discarded, I was able to design my garden. We planted an abundance of drought-tolerant plants and added a fountain. The mosaics are from Mosaic House, New York, and the pot from Inner Gardens.

ABOVE In the sitting room, my mother's 19th-century English writing desk is home to some of my favorite photos. The Frank Stella print that hangs above was bought by Gary before we were married. I had the generous Irish linen damask curtains made from a discounted weave that was in the collection.

ABOVE RIGHT The Hunt Slonem painting has pride of place above the sofa and is the visual centerpiece of the room. The English club fender was made in my atelier in LA, while the various fabrics are from my Mexico Meets Morocco collection. The 19th-century French gilt mirror came from Rosemarie McCaffrey Antiques & Interiors in Santa Monica.

While living here, I launched my first fabric collection and from then on our home became a testing ground for new designs—the boys rarely returned from school to find a piece of furniture in the same place as it had occupied in the morning. Most of all, this house was where my many different roles all came together—wife and mother, designer, hostess, gardener, and dog walker. And it was where I finally had a bedroom with high enough ceilings to indulge in a secret wish—a canopied four-poster bed hung with fringed curtains, piled high with pillows, and, more often than not, occupied by my three young sons, jumping, wriggling, and squealing with laughter. This house began as a dream, and ended as one.

The simple Shaker-style kitchen has wall shelves rather than cabinets. My treasured collection of Bauer Pottery includes both original and reproduction pieces. The claret AGA stove picks up on the Roman shades in my Abu design in Red Currant.

ABOVE In my bedroom, the chair and ottoman are covered in my Moroccan Stripe fabric in Silvertree, while the Kashmiri side table came from India many moons ago. The standing lamp was found on London's Lillie Road.

RIGHT The huge French 19th-century mirror is from The Furniture Cave, London and the Chesterfield sofa was also sourced in England, but so long ago that I can't remember exactly where. The enveloping, luxurious bed curtains are my Lola fabric in Rose Coral.

LEFT AND ABOVE The custom-made bed was designed and made in my workshop and dressed with my woven Sheer Stripe in Green. All the fabrics and the wallpaper in this room come from my Mexico Meets Morocco collection. The low table was sourced at Berbere in Los Angeles and the Moroccan rug came from Amadi Carpets. The assorted knicknacks all came home with me from various travels.

BELOW AND OPPOSITE I knew that I wanted our outside space to be lush, abundant and secluded, reminiscent of the gardens of a Spanish finca or Moroccan riad. My vision was brought to life by my friend Stephen Block, who also happens to be a renowned landscaper (see his home on pages 36–49). The table and benches, the scene of so many happy, lively meals with family and friends, came from Stephen's company Inner Gardens.

Serious is not a word that should be used in decorating—the unexpected is a must.

LA LA LAND

Not long before the pandemic struck, I was invited to dinner at the Los Angeles home of Bob and Susie Wallerstein. They are great hosts and their mix of interesting guests and excellent food and wine always results in a fun evening. It wasn't long before I got chatting with one of my fellow guests, an Academy Award-nominated British actor. It just so happened that he was looking for someone to update his Hollywood Hills home, and our hostess Susie had recommended me. Little did we know that Covid-19 was already lurking offstage.

A few days later, I showed my prospective client around my house and we chatted about the redesign of his LA base. After a hilarious afternoon, he left laden with books and fabrics to look at, and I was thrilled to to be given the task of updating his Spanish Colonial Revival home that dated from the 1920s. Los Angeles is awash with buildings in this style, which became almost ubiquitous in the early decades of the 20th-century. Plastered walls, decorative tile, arched windows and doorways, and wrought-iron fixtures are all hallmarks of the style, which evokes all the heritage and romance of California. Sadly, many of these houses have been torn down or insensitively updated, destroying their original charm. It's very upsetting.

Despite an enviable location, this house had undergone some unfortunate updates. While it had once enjoyed a bucolic one-acre setting, the plot had since been subdivided and the house now lacked the privacy of its earlier years. However, there was a lovely garden and, although the kitchen and bathrooms needed repair, I could see that their period charm could be resurrected. The house felt like a neglected beauty, and I was eager to return her to her former glory. My client had been living with the tired décor, but was ready to get to work on a revamp. We both relished the prospect of restoring the historic detailing of the property while creating a comfortable and colorful home. His only ask was that his collection of artworks be given pride of place in the redesigned interior. These paintings were treasured possessions and provided the inspiration for each room's color story.

During lockdown, construction was deemed an essential endeavor, so on-site structural work, which included the reinstallation of lost fireplaces as well as a remodeled kitchen and two bathrooms, proceeded while the world stayed at home. I created simple yet colorful window treatments and introduced a generous dollop of pattern and upholstery. Despite the best efforts of the coronavirus, I was able to deliver on my promise to create a comfortable Californian home and adorn it with the art collection of a globetrotting actor, all the while righting the wrongs that had been inflicted on this charming piece of Spanish Colonial Revival architecture.

PAGE 88 In the light, sunny sitting room, the focal point is the painting over the sofa by Sebastiano Ciarcia. The pillows were custom-made, and the lamps and side tables are from The Perfect Room. The client already owned the chair, and I had it recovered in a vibrant Pakistani ralli quilt. The bowl and coffee table came home with me from Marrakech.

LEFT A reading nook is home to a print of Picasso's *Mains aux Fleurs*. The fabrics on the bench cushion (Tangier) and pillow (Fez Palm) are from my Mexico Meets Morocco collection.

BELOW Art by Sebastiano Ciarcia. The floor-length curtains are in my Fez Palm print in Electric Blue.

OPPOSITE The pair of English lamps are by KMI Studio with lampshades custom-made in KMI ticking. A desk from Christopher Hodsoll is paired with an iron chair from Martyn Lawrence Bullard. The carpet is from Vandra Rugs.

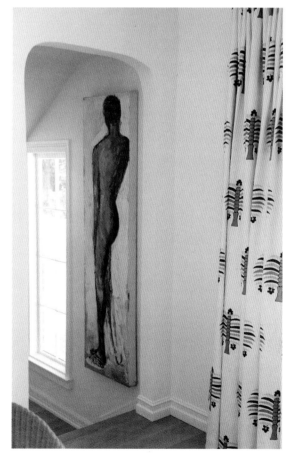

ABOVE AND RIGHT In the music room, the custom-made sofa is KMI Studio and the Moroccan octagonal coffee table came from Berbere in LA. The colourful rug was found at Amadi Carpets. The painting over the sofa was from the client's collection.

OPPOSITE I found the drop-shaped mirror in the Moroccan district in Marseille. The lamp and the cricket table beside the bed came from The Perfect Room, while the headboard was custom-made for the room. My trademark dashes of red bring the scheme to life.

OPPOSITE ABOVE With the help of my brother Robert and his team of expert tradespeople, we were able to renovate in a timely manner. Antique French doors lead to the ensuite bathroom.

OPPOSITE In the bathroom, the Roman blinds are Wilson Stripe Sage from Otis Textiles. The porcelain tile came from Classic Tile in Santa Monica, and the bathtub and faucets are from Snyder Diamond in Santa Monica. I had the charming little early 20th-century French chair reupholstered in Scottish Hampton Blues from Otis Textiles.

LEFT AND BELOW The cushion cover is an original Moroccan weaving from my vintage textiles collection. I had the bedcover made up in my Natural Marrakech fabric in Teal. The dark wood bobbin bed looks like an antique but in fact came from The Perfect Room. The Roman blinds and curtain are in Genghis, which is hand-woven and embroidered in Marrakech and the carpet is by Vandra Rugs.

BRIEF ENCOUNTER

One day, out of the blue, a couple from London made an unsolicited offer to buy my 18th Street home (see pages 76–87). The offer came with a condition—I had to make an immediate decision and be out by the end of the month. This was the biggest quandary I had faced since I first landed in Los Angeles. It had taken me two decades to burnish and tweak this property to perfection; I had raised three boys here and it was filled with memories. But the boys were at college or building independent lives, and I was itching for a new adventure. Though the timing was not ideal and the logistics of clearing out were overwhelming, I agreed to sell.

When I dipped my toe back into the real-estate market, I discovered exactly why my buyers had dangled their unsolicited cash offer in my face. There were too many buyers chasing too few houses, resulting in bidding wars for mediocre properties. So I followed the advice I always gave to friends facing a crossroads: when in doubt, go to France. I decamped to my home there, telling myself I'd resume the hunt on my return to LA a few months later.

I decided that my next address would be a transition home, a holdover. Rather than throwing money away on a rental, I needed somewhere to live and to park my money while I contemplated my next move. With this in mind, I ended up attending the open houses of the generic spec homes that were proliferating across the Westside. I was a motivated buyer who wanted to close quickly on a turnkey property, a house that did not require renovation. Being an interior designer, I knew I could work with any blank architectural canvas. And that is exactly what I found in Venice Beach.

I closed on a brand-new house walking distance from the Pacific Ocean. Its clean and streamlined aesthetic was not a natural fit for me, but the house was ready to move into and also all to my taste. I bought the house because of the statuesque California live oak that dominated the garden and could be seen from the master bedroom—this clinched the deal for me. The beachside neighborhood was charming, and the location was just ten minutes from my new offices, which were now doubling as a design and production facility for my fabric enterprise and the beginnings of my tech company The Perfect Room.

My new home could not accommodate all the furnishings and treasures that had occupied 18th Street, but editing the contents turned out to be a good exercise. It was unusual for me to subtract rather than add, but at the same time it was fun to try something new. The stakes were not high, as I knew Venice was a detour from the next steps. It was a great house to live in and a perfect pitstop. Looking back, I'm very happy to have had my "Venice moment."

PAGE 96 Standing on the doorstep of my gap-year home in Venice, CA, where I took up paddleboarding and surfing just to impress the boys. The house benefited from a few finishing touches: fabric, art, and my lifelong collection of furniture. Any home can capture who you are by the things you bring with you from place to place, such as these flowerpots from 18th Street. The front door was painted in my favorite blue from Benjamin Moore.

OPPOSITE Julian Chichester's classic Dakota table has long been a staple in homes with small dining rooms. Mine is covered with my collection of candlesticks. The dining chairs from the Albi flea market in south west France have been so much admired over the years that I now make my own version. The light fixture was from Obsolete in Mar Vista, a go-to for all vintage and antique lighting. The wall sconces were bought originally for Steve Martin, but with nowhere to put them in his home, eventually they ended up in my house. I never buy anything for a client that I wouldn't want for myself— it's my number one rule.

RIGHT The spacious hallway is light-filled thanks to the large picture windows above the front door. The bench and console table were both bought at the flea market in Albi, France. The house served its purpose and was featured in both *House Beautiful* and *Homes & Gardens*.

PAGES 100–101 My furniture from 18th Street fit perfectly here, although I gave all the soft furnishings a fabric facelift with new slipcovers to introduce new textiles and colorways of some favorite prints. Sheer curtains diffuse the Californian light.

OPPOSITE The industrial lighting over the counter came from Obsolete. I took out the cascading waterfall of marble, which just reeked of 'spec', and replaced it with Caesarstone as it is the most durable option and great to look at, too. The boys' portraits were taken by Marie-Laure de Decker, one of France's most eminent photographers. It's the accessories that bring your personality to every room, so collecting and keeping these valuable memories is a must.

RIGHT The importance of books should never be underestimated. The Swedish leather chair came from Obsolete. Bowls from the Languedoc region in France, once used for making confit, are both decorative and useful. The Moroccan rug was brought back from a trip to Marrakech.

LEFT In every house I've lived in, there has to be an outstanding feature. Here it was the California live oak tree that took center stage from the bedroom window. My favorite curtains from my bedroom on 18th Street were luckily a perfect fit. Fabrics from my British Isles collection were used to re-cover all the soft furnishings in this room— the paisley design on the headboard is Kirkbean. The Judy Greenwood standing lamp, which I inherited from my friends Corbin Bernsen and Amanda Pays, still remains in my bedroom, as do the bedside tables from Charles Jacobsen in Culver City.

ABOVE The bathrooms in this house were another reason to outbid all the other offers. The paneled walls here were repainted a soft green-grey to complement Roman shades in Bouquet from my British Isles collection. On the Waterworks etagere rests a painting that the late Louise Fletcher (best known for playing Nurse Ratched in *One Flew Over the Cuckoo's Nest*) gave me for my birthday one year.

THIS PAGE KMI Studio's queen-size bed works perfectly in this guest bedroom. My signature look of throwing my Sheer Stripe over a bedframe dresses it just enough. The vintage Kashmiri side table came from Vaughan.

OPPOSITE A French chaise is covered in Greta Blue from my Batik collection. The curtain and bedcover fabric, Egerton from the British Isles collection, is one of my favorites. All rooms must have a dash of red, if not a lot!

There's always a reason to buy a house, and in this case it was the live California oak tree in the garden.

OPPOSITE The garden offered a variety of seating areas in which to sit and enjoy the Californian weather. Here, vintage French iron chairs surround a table covered by a cloth in Kirkbean Red in Turquoise. The design was named after the remote fishing village where I grew up, on the Solway Coast in Scotland.

RIGHT An Indian bedspread doubles as a tablecloth in the garden. Suspended from the tree, wicker lanterns from Inner Garden brought the garden to life at night.

MEXICO MEETS MOROCCO

While working on a project in California, I fell in love with the fabrics of Mexico and Morocco. Intrigued by the bold patterns and lively colors native to both countries, I wanted to design a collection that married the two cultures.

THE GREAT REVIVAL

One Sunday, over coffee and the *Los Angeles Times* real estate section, I came upon a listing for an early 20th-century property in Ojai, a hippie hamlet an hour's drive north of Santa Monica. What caught my eye was the inclusion of my two favorite phrases: 'needs restoration' and 'stables'.

The building itself was a pastiche of a Mexican hacienda with Tudor additions, oozing with charm. It was originally built by glass magnate Edward Libbey, a Midwesterner who bought a vast amount of land and developed what is today the Ojai Valley Inn as a private golf course for friends and family. In 1923, he commissioned architect Wallace Neff to design and construct a stable block. However, on Libbey's death in 1925, the ranch passed into the hands of a new owner, and another notable architect, Austen Pierpont, stepped in to reconfigure the house and stables into a summer residence for Baltimore native William Lucking. Under Lucking's direction, Pierpont embellished the enclave with Tudor-style additions, and this is how it remains today.

The compound is built in materials from the Ojai Valley—colossal river stones, rough-hewn timbers, and traditional adobe bricks. But the ravages of time had taken their toll, and the Libbey Ranch I first encountered was in a state of disrepair. Even worse, it was a prime candidate for demolition. The market had remained indifferent toward the steep price tag for more than three years; no one, not even Diane Keaton, wanted to take it on.

Before I had completed my first walk-through, I knew I would save the place. Two homes on two different continents was proving to be too much even for me to keep up with, and if I had thrown my French house and Santa Monica home into a blender, out would come Libbey Ranch. I acquired the property and plunged right in. However, having planned a speedy six-month project, I was to be knee-deep in adobe conservation for the next year. The 5,000sq.ft./464sq.m. structure required some reconfiguration, which is my forte. Eliminating interior hallways, overhauling the kitchen, and putting in much-needed bathrooms were essential. The rest of the house just needed some sympathetic restoration. The jewel-like tiles and red oak flooring were cleaned up, and I restored the authentic Talavera tiled stair, which led up to a mezzanine and a

PAGES 112 AND 113 The courtyard was pulled apart—an existing dead tree was removed and I had a large pot installed for a fountain in its place. I love the trickle of water. The external paint color was specially mixed to match the original color.

LEFT The bar cart, originally from Sicily, was found at Rosemarie McCaffrey Antiques & Interiors in Santa Monica. One of my favorite pieces, it travels with me from house to house. The candlestick-turned-lamp came from Dos Gallos in Los Angeles.

OPPOSITE All the ironwork on the property was made here in the forge. The painting of a Spanish lady was bought in Ojai—I saw it propped canvas-side out against a wall and told the store owner I'd take it before even seeing the subject matter. The high-ceilinged hallway turned out to be the perfect home for her.

Juliet balcony. Locally, I sourced period furniture and lighting fixtures that complemented the original ironwork drapery rods, door hardware, banisters, and balustrades that had all been forged on the property. The house turned out to be a wonderful backdrop for my textile designs, which I used for draperies, pillows, and bedding.

For months, my team lived on site and the house, which had sat for many years dormant and neglected, basked in much-needed love and attention. Once finished, the ranch was such a masterpiece that it featured in both *Vogue* and *House Beautiful*, and I ultimately sold it to an A-list actress. Although the house was not to be mine forever, it was mine to restore.

LEFT An assortment of riding gear decorates the hat rack. The huge pieces of river rock used to accentuate the archway were all found here on the property.

OPPOSITE The simple Shaker-style kitchen, with wall shelves rather than cabinets, is my go-to design and one you'll see in many of my houses. The design never dates and works in all styles of home.

LEFT AND ABOVE The guest bedrooms charmingly accommodate multiple beds. Painting out the wood in these rooms gave them an immediate update.

OPPOSITE More river rock was used by Pierpont in the 1930s to construct walls, fireplaces, and hallways. The carpet came from Amadi Carpets in West Hollywood.

Combining a check, a stripe, and a floral is my recipe for success.

RIGHT The boys, now teenagers, were reluctant to leave their friends, school, and Santa Monica beaches, so I had to come up with all sorts of fun ideas at weekends in order to lure them up here without complaints. However, Oscar, my oldest son, is soon to be married in Ojai, and when revisiting the property recently was filled with remorse that they hadn't seen the possibilities of this glorious ranch all those years ago. The photo was taken by Dewey Nicks for *Vogue*.

FAR FROM THE MADDING CROWD

t's always an honor to be recommended to clients by an architect of record, especially one whom I admire as much as my friend and collaborator Marc Appleton. Marc has designed and restored a host of eminent estates up and down the California coast during the course of his award-winning career. As a child, he spent vacations and holidays at his grandparents' home Florestal, one of Santa Barbara's finest Spanish Colonial Revival homes designed by the eminent architect George Washington Smith.

Marc introduced me to a couple who were enamored of his redesign of the San Ysidro Ranch, where I had worked with him on the model rooms. They had recently acquired an avocado ranch in Ventura County overlooking the ocean. The existing 1990s ranch house on site was of little architectural merit, but having visited the Libbey Ranch in Ojai (see pages 112–121), the couple were adamant that this property should be all about the land and the views and to leave the house alone! As they had bought it fully furnished, I was simply to update the interiors, adding fabrics, pillows, lampshades, and throws to enhance the inherited pieces.

My client has an incredible eye for finding extraordinary property. A cosmetic maven, she is the best editor, and without her I wouldn't have had the bandwidth to transform this property so successfully. I was given from Labor Day to Thanksgiving for my "zhuzh." This "zhuzh," however, turned into remodeling bathrooms, airfreighting tiles from Morocco, stripping floors, and generally bringing soul to the house. The property was crying out for color, paint, and window treatments, and I added beautiful vintage Mexican tiles as well as geometric and intricately patterned Moroccan tiles with saturated glazes to create unique bathrooms.

By the time the clients arrived for Thanksgiving, the building resembled a South American hacienda that had been there for a hundred years, with antique tile embedded into the walls, Spanish light fixtures, and European furnishings. I had planted dozens of terracotta pots around the bougainvillea-fringed courtyard, while inside we had created coved ceilings, arched doorways, and built-in bookcases. In tune with the architecture, I introduced wrought-iron hardware, vintage lights, colorful pillows, and fabrics from my Mexico Meets Morocco collection.

PAGE 122 The clients' own chairs were re-covered in leather from Ashbury Hides. The coffee table is from William Laman and the the mirror and inlaid tiles from Michael Haskell Antiques.

OPPOSITE A custom wall color by Olivia Raeburn and fabrics by Robert Kime help recreate the feel of old Mexico. The rustic chandelier and Mexican cupboard are both from 1stDibs.

ABOVE A bespoke bench from KMI Studio was upholstered in Entrelacs by Le Manach from Claremont. On the shelves, a drawing by Diego Rivera is seen with 16th- and 17th-century artifacts from around the globe.

The floors were a mix of terracotta Mexican pavers and refinished hardwood, with area rugs to keep the colorful motif rolling from room to room. I was given carte blanche to take risks that most people wouldn't have the foresight to appreciate. The 18th-century Swedish fisherman's table in the kitchen, which I found on 1stDibs, was the most expensive item I bought for the house. Most people want to put their money in the living room over the mantelpiece, but I believe that spending in unorthodox places often leads to the success of a house.

After remodeling the ranch-style home, which was to be the clients' main residence,

I continued to work alongside Marc on the various workers' trailer homes, which we turned into one- and two-bedroom cottages. With the help of landscape architect Art Luna, the trailers were transformed and the instant gardens that Art created gave the final touches to this spectacular property.

This project was another labour of love. My team and I had remodeled and successfully decorated the house in time for Thanksgiving dinner. Drawing on the tight schedules of my film production days, in three months we were able to complete the project. The crew lived on site and I hired a catering company to feed them.

LEFT Character was brought to the kitchen by refacing the cupboards with star cutouts and adding a Moroccan tile backsplash. Reproduction Bauer Pottery mingles with antique Mexican and Moroccan bowls and cut-glass French bottles. The 18th-century Swedish fish-cutting table, from Dienst + Dotter Antikviteter in New York, took six men to set in place.

BELOW A painting by Laura Fiume, found at R E Steele Antiques in East Hampton, hangs above a reclaimed mantel from a salvage yard in Northern California. The inlaid tiles are from Exquisite Surfaces in Beverly Hills.

OPPOSITE The curtains for the master bedroom hallway were made from vintage Mexican serapes from Michael Haskell Antiques along with the wooden chairs. The quirky light fixtures are from the Blanchard Collective in Marlborough, England and the floor runners are from Amadi Carpets in West Hollywood.

ABOVE AND OPPOSITE French designer Jacques Adnet's 1950s desk and
chair live comfortably with an Anglo-Indian bed from Robert Kime, and
a late 17th-century Flemish armoire. Tibetan horns repurposed as lamps
from Pat McGann Gallery in West Hollywood sit on reproduction
nightstands from Rooms & Gardens. The combination of these pieces in
a United Nations of decorating illustrates that time or country of origin is
not important—it's knowing where things go that creates the harmony in
a room. No one item should shout out at you.

RIGHT The Moroccan tiles that line the shower are from Mosaic House in
New York. The colorful rug is from Pat McGann Gallery. The vintage chair
has been re-covered with a Pakistani ralli quilt; both were found at The
Rose Bowl in Pasadena.

OPPOSITE One of the guest bedrooms is an array of pinks and florals—Pierre Frey curtains, a chaise upholstered in Bombay by Raoul Textiles, and a John Robshaw bedcover. The Portuguese bed was found in pieces and rebuilt in my workshop. Olivia Raeburn hand-painted the walls.

ABOVE The greatest challenge was to make this 1990s ranch-style house look as though it dated from the 1890s. Chairs, tables, and hammocks from Dos Gallos in West Hollywood create comfortable seating areas under the loggias. Chandeliers enhance the nighttime atmosphere.

BROADCAST NEWS

was first introduced to my friend Mark Robertson by our great mutual friend and my fellow interior designer Barry Dixon, who has worked with Mark on various of his homes over the years. Having collaborated with such prominent designers, Mark has developed a practiced eye and over the years has become an accomplished designer himself.

Living in New York, Mark needs to escape from city life and the high drama of his job producing celebrity content for *Good Morning America*. For many years, he owned a house in Southampton—a beautifully finished and furnished getaway. During one stay with him, I pulled out my fabric swatches, which I always seem to have on hand, and together we selected all the finishing touches in the shape of window treatments, bedcovers, and the odd throw pillow. After this icing on the cake, the home was perfection. However, during Covid, Mark received an offer on the house that he could not refuse. Luckily, it was not too much of a wrench—he already had itchy feet and had been contemplating a move to the eastern part of Long Island to be closer to friends.

After exchanging endless texts discussing various listings with Barry and me, Mark fell in love with his next Hamptons retreat. It is located in Springs, just outside of East Hampton, where artists have lived for many decades—most notably Jackson Pollock and Lee Krasner—and which has so far resisted the trend toward the development of large, lavish houses. The area is quiet, low-key, and reminiscent of the Amagansett of my early twenties. The most exciting part was that the house was "move-in ready," as the previous owners had carefully renovated the property to give it the additional square footage it badly needed. Fortunately, this had been done without taking away any of its original 1920s charm.

Even with a house that is move-in ready, there are always things one has to do in order to make it one's own. Mark knows exactly what he likes, but he also knows when he needs a little help. He had sold the window treatments and many of the furnishings to the buyer of his Southampton house, so the two of us needed to shop for a few specific pieces, then elevate the overall scheme with paint, wallpaper, and fabric from my latest collection.

PAGES 132 AND 133 The walls of the entrance hall are papered in my Leaves design in Red, which complements the Roman shade in Ottoman Stripe from my Jewels of the East collection. The lamp is from John Blazey Vintage in Miami.

THIS PAGE The kitchen island and barstools were painted a vibrant teal. Two pictures from Robert Steele hang by the window. The basket over the stove is from Nickey Kehoe and an antique suzani was repurposed as a door curtain.

Mark knows that one of my greatest skills as an interior decorator is that I understand the importance of comfort—my houses are always supremely comfortable as well as beautiful. When I visited Mark's new home, my weekend jobs were to help him choose fabrics, paint colors, and additional pieces that would give the house the "Kathryn" touches that he has come to love, having spent many a summer as my houseguest at La Castellane. On his many visits to France, he had bought ceramic pots, bronze busts, and various knicknacks at the local antiques fairs. Mark is one of the few people I know who loves antiquing as much as I do. Both of us would forego a Michelin-starred five-course meal in favor of being the first in line to view the latest spoils from our favorite shops, Laurin Copen Antiques in Bridgehampton and Ruby Beets and Katie Leede in Sag Harbor. Half the fun of working with Mark is going on these shopping excursions together.

By the time I had worked my magic on this house, it was ready for Mark's first summer guests to arrive. I was thrilled when Mark decided to move—I was looking forward to helping him create a place that I could also visit and enjoy with my family. With Mark's favorite pieces from his previous house and the new purchases we had made together, the house was going to be an idyllic home away from home in the Hamptons for me too.

OPPOSITE A light fixture from Obsolete hangs above the dining table, which is surrounded by distinctive orange chairs from Barry Dixon.

ABOVE RIGHT On a bar cart from John Blazey Vintage is a lamp with shade from Katie Leede in Sag Harbor.

PAGES 138–139 In the living room, the coffee table is home to a small bronze sculpture by Claude Palmier and a ceramic pot that I found in France. The wicker chair and white standing lamp are from Homenature. The mirror came from JED Design and Antiques. My Togo Check fabric was used for the Roman shade.

OPPOSITE A headboard, pillow, and curtains in my Bouquet pattern in Blue are teamed with a bedcover in Dalbeattie Blue and a lampshade from Katie Leede & Co on a table from Laurin Copen Antiques.

RIGHT The bathroom wallpaper is my Lilac design in Green. There are various accessories on the counter from R E Steele in East Hampton.

BELOW The master bedroom soft furnishings were made using my Hand Stitched Multi and Indian Mirror Multi, with the exception of hand-dyed pillows from Kirsten Hecktermann and an armchair reupholstered in my Zig Zag Red.

Mark knows that I understand the importance of comfort.

OPPOSITE The guest bathroom's wood paneling was painted in a russet red from Farrow & Ball, chosen to tie in with the existing tile. Mark bought the sailor portraits locally.

ABOVE The simple but inviting guest bedroom next door has a headboard and Roman shades in Egerton Paisley Red and striped bedcovers from Otis Textiles.

ON THE WATERFRONT

When I received a phone call from an unknown man calling from an unknown number to say that my house in France had really caught his eye because it didn't look decorated, I wasn't quite sure whether to take it as a compliment or an insult.

At the back of my mind, I wondered whether this was for real or a prank call from one of my friends, but I followed my instincts and continued to listen. Just as well. It turned out that the praise was sincere, the prospect of a job was serious, and the whole thing was, as my sons would say, "totally legit."

My new clients were about to break ground on a new home built on the same spot as their home of many years. I was working on the East Coast at the time, and arranged to drive up to meet them. They were long-time Hamptons residents, well-known and well-liked in the community—both had played a leading role in revitalizing the waterfront and keeping Sag Harbor true to its historic roots.

The couple traveled a great deal and were looking for an experienced interior designer who could handle everything, from soup to nuts. They had seen my work in *Elle Decor* when Margaret Russell, the then editor-in-chief, did a career-changing piece on my house in France and liked my style—sophisticated yet family friendly, comfortable, and not too precious. As a result, my clients' request couldn't have been more straightforward: "Just do what you do." I had enough projects and press under my belt to impress them, so they put themselves in my hands and trusted me and my team. We shook hands on a budget, and I jumped right in.

Fellow Hamptons resident and architect Frank Greenwald had worked with the clients as the project developed from a single-story home into a year-round residence set on a breathtaking piece of property overlooking Long Island Sound. Frank's design included an office, a library, and a large family great room. He oriented the principal wings of the house perfectly to capture views of the water from every room. I loved working with Frank, along with Jeff Gagliotti from the Hamptons-based contractor Bulgin & Associates. We were something of a dream team, and having those two to show me the way meant that I quickly picked up the language of the architect and contractor and got to see how a house was built. This was to be the first house that I was involved in, built from the ground up!

PAGE 144 The house had more places to sit than to sleep, so in the upstairs sitting room I positioned a pair of chaises for napping. The curtains are a Bennison fabric.

ABOVE The dining table and chairs were custom-made by my studio and the chairs upholstered in a Colefax & Fowler fabric. The chandelier and mirror are from Daniel Mankowitz in London.

RIGHT The antique coffer was bought on a trip to Guatemala, the Corinthian Column lamps came from Vaughan, and the lampshades from William Yeoward. The painting over the fireplace came from an antiques market in Connecticut.

With clients that trusted me implicitly, this job was a joy. In my usual frugal way, I shopped at out-of-the-way places far from all the usual furniture stores, sourcing antiques in London and Paris and from Hudson to Connecticut. When designing the sofas and chairs, I mixed in fabrics from my Quilt and Toile collections with velvets from Claremont, Bennison florals, and tartans from Anta.

Today, the house remains just as sophisticated and timeless as the day it was finished. A few years ago, I gave the house a refresh while working on a family wedding—it was a pleasure to revisit and give it some additional love.

ABOVE The huge kitchen, which stretches the full depth of the house, has Roman shades in my Ikat Check Sage and custom knobs from McKinney & Co.

RIGHT The walls of the downstairs bathroom were hand-painted by Olivia Raeburn. The Venetian-inspired octagonal mirror came from Julian Chichester.

OPPOSITE The sunroom is curtained with Sheer Stripe in Sage, while the seating is upholstered in Ikat Green. Lamps from Daniel Mankowitz are teamed with shades from Vaughan.

ABOVE When faced with the prospect of filling a large, blank wall, I like to take many family photos and put them in different-size frames made from the same color wood for a cohesive display.

RIGHT The oversize lanterns on the wall are from the Blanchard Collective, Marlborough, England. The table came from my own home—it was a piece that I never wanted to part with, but seeing that it was a perfect fit for this hallway, I knew I had to let it go. The bronze bulls by Peter Woytuk are small versions of the ones belonging to The Hotchkiss School in Lakeville, Connecticut. My client loved the originals so much that the artist made miniature ones for her.

A splash of red is uplifting and brings every room good luck.

OPPOSITE For the master bedroom, I chose a palette of soft, serene colors enlivened by vibrant splashes of red. The antique Chinese cupboard came from Charles Jacobsen in Los Angeles.

RIGHT The center table in the bathroom was bought from John Heaton Antiques. The slipper chair is upholstered in Floral Blue from my first collection, and the ceiling pendant is from Vaughan.

SOMETHING'S GOTTA GIVE

This 1820s farmhouse in Amagansett, Long Island started as a remodeling job, but turned into a rebuild along the way. Years of salt water and Atlantic gales had rotted the wooden framework of the beautiful old farmhouse, which had to be taken down to the studs and rebuilt from the ground up. At this point, my clients Andy and Kari Lyn Sabin brought local architect Francis Fleetwood on board to redesign what was left of the house, incorporating as best he could its historic footprint and features.

As the Sabins are year-round residents, I didn't want their house to have a Hamptons coastal theme. Rather, I wanted to keep the interiors true to the 19th-century original construction—a traditional American style, the kind of home that might be seen up the Hudson or in Connecticut. My vision was traditional but still fresh, relaxed, and suitable for family life.

I used a selection of fabrics from my Quilt and Toile collections as the basis for a palette of muted harvest tones that would be easy on the eye and attractive in every season. The boldest use of color is in the family room next to the kitchen, which I painted a tomato red, completing the scheme with a classic Bennison floral print, plus curtains in an oversize red check. The dining area took shape when I sourced a set of late 18th-century American ladder-back chairs, while the large table was custom-made by local woodworker Charles DeSapio of Country Gear. Antique Dutch-style brass chandeliers and sconces original to the house add luster throughout.

Kari Lyn, who is Texas born and a former model, was always up for a challenge. She and I worked on this project with the same contractor as the house shown on pages 144–153, and the three of us made a formidable team. With incredible foresight, Kari Lyn had salvaged every piece of original door hardware during the rebuild, which anchored the new house to its predecessor. She had also salvaged much of the original hardwood flooring, and this was patched together with other salvaged timber to create gracious, wide-plank wooden floors.

PAGE 155 The Ikat Check Red curtains dominate this room. Paired with a sofa upholstered in a Bennison floral and a Cowtan & Tout stripe, they used up my quota for color and pattern.

RIGHT We managed to save the wide-plank floors, which are original to the house. The dining table was custom-made to go with the ladder-back chairs. Kari Lyn and I found the painting in East Hampton.

When it came to furnishings, I was in my element shopping on the East Coast. One of my pet peeves is when people furnish a house entirely from a design center, choosing reproductions that won't stand the test of time. Antiques, upcycling, and reusing are so much more interesting, after all.

With two houses now under my belt in the Hamptons, and my colorful new fabric collections, I was very much flavor of the month. As an interior decorator, I know the importance of combining different patterns and my mantra is that using a check, a stripe, and a floral is the key to a harmonious room.

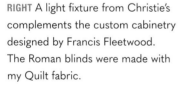

RIGHT A light fixture from Christie's complements the custom cabinetry designed by Francis Fleetwood. The Roman blinds were made with my Quilt fabric.

RIGHT The pieces in this room are a mixture of the Sabins' own and new pieces we selected together. The sofas and ottoman were custom-made in my Los Angeles workshop and upholstered in Ikat Tan from my first collection.

"Her sense of proportion, color, and the reality of our lifestyle makes Kathryn's rooms feel alive, inviting, and livable."—
Kari Lyn Sabin

BELOW All the fixtures in the bathrooms throughout the house came from Waterworks. The fabric on the custom ottoman and curtains is Sheer Stripe Blue.

RIGHT The bed hangings are lined with Ikat Blue and the outer fabric is my staple cream-colored crewelwork from Chelsea Textiles with a Colefax & Fowler trim.

OPPOSITE A reclaimed mantel from the original house is paired with a ship painting found at R E Steele Antiques in East Hampton. The rug is from Woodard & Greenstein.

TOILE

My philosophy for combining patterns and colors in a room is that there should always be a floral, a stripe, and a check. With this in mind, I put a new spin on these designs with hints of European and Asian influences.

HIGH SOCIETY

While my tenure on Bravo TV's *Million Dollar Decorators* was a career high with regard to exposure, the production timetable for the show only accelerated the frantic pace of my professional life—constant travel for meetings with clients and to oversee ongoing projects alongside the exhaustive preparation that the fabric collections entailed. I craved a pause and assumed that when the second season wrapped, my life would wind down.

But that was not to be, and I found myself wondering how I could pivot my business to accommodate more clients but with less time and travel involved. This was how the idea of my design retreats was born—an ingenious new concept to point homeowners in the right direction yet without committing to a costly full interior design package. To my amazement the concept took off and I was suddenly booking long weekends in Santa Monica and week-long retreats at my house in southern France.

This new departure was my entrée to one of the great sporting families of America, the Rooneys, and gave birth to wonderful friendships and fabulous houses to design. One day, a woman called to book a retreat for her, her sisters, and her mother, all of whom had a house undergoing a redesign. The woman was Bridget Rooney, and the house was a Cape Cod property she had recently purchased from the estate of the inestimably stylish Bunny Mellon.

Once the ladies arrived in Los Angeles, my team and I workshopped rooms for each of them, and by the end of the weekend, as they left clutching their moodboards, we had all become fast friends. In the midst of the goodbyes, Bridget suddenly announced that it would be more fun if she and I did her new house together. And that is how I ended up taking a crack at an iconic property with the brief being to give it a sympathetic overhaul.

Despite the house's pedigree, the structure was far more understated than I had expected. The location was extraordinary—private, discreet, comfortable, and unpretentious. I loved it.

PAGES 166 AND 167 The garden house is a Bunny Mellon design that appears in various properties that she owned (page 166). The entrance hall has its original hand-painted checkerboard floors, which were touched up wherever necessary (page 167).

THIS PAGE The living room, which overlooks the estuary, was painted a soft blue with my two-tone Solway sheers at the windows. The soft blue-green weave on the chairs is from my collection for Scalamandré. The sofa on the left is covered in my Moroccan Stripe in Silvertree, while the one to the right is Abu in Cream. The coffee table is from my Pied à Terre collection and the carpet is from Vandra Rugs.

THIS PAGE Bridget and I found these Swedish chairs in her storage unit and Lief in Los Angeles made a table to match. The timeless Swedish serpentine commode was also the clients' own, as are the paintings hanging throughout the house, including this one by August Herbin, a French artist known for his abstract paintings.

OPPOSITE A view down the corridor that spans the width of the house to the formal dining room. Mrs Mellon's original floors are still intact, although we carried out some minor repair work. To the right of the door is a nude by Milton Avery, while the landscape over the fireplace in the dining room is a Grant Wood.

As luck would have it, the purchase of the house included a handful of the furnishings and accessories that had long lived within it, and Bridget and her husband had a warehouse full of extraordinary pieces that fitted the house like a glove. To fill any gaps, we met in Palm Beach for a shopping trip with Bridget's sisters Maggie and Kathleen and her mother June, which was more fun than furniture. As it turned out, these ladies all loved a good yard sale and rummaging through the shops on Dixie Highway.

Bridget had an exceptional team in place to implement the necessary upgrades that were needed at the estate and the work was soon completed. Working from the moodboards we had brainstormed together in LA, and with the veritable trove of warehouse furnishings, Bridget and I installed our Palm Beach finds alongside pieces that had always been there and interwove a soft, breezy palette of paint, wallpaper, and linens from my collection to welcome inside the sun-faded tones of the New England beachscape just outside. And apart from a simple coat of paint, I left Mrs. Mellon's original kitchen absolutely untouched.

Bridget and I had a blast together—she and her husband adored the finished results and we have gone on to work together on several subsequent projects. The finished house was a triumph, and proof of this was a comment from a former member of Bunny's staff who had spent many years at the beach house. As she apprehended the scope of the redesign, she turned to me and announced, "Mrs. Mellon would have approved of this."

"With Kathryn's help, we tried to preserve much of Bunny Mellon's original design aesthetic. It is casual and elegant: a truly special place in our family's heart. Bunny love!"—

Bridget Rooney

LEFT The fabulous upholstered settee in its original tapestry came from an auction at Sotheby's. Two classic Vaughan standing lamps flank the piece.

ABOVE One day, Bridget bounced in and said "Let's paint the floor red!" She certainly got some ideas from my design retreat! The throw on the chair is my Dalbeattie design.

LEFT We kept all the original existing bathroom fittings but redecorated to give the rooms a refresh. The wallcovers are Greta Reverse Green with Roses Red on the chair.

OPPOSITE This tiny, cosy bedroom, where I sleep when visiting, has wonderful views across the water. The headboard and bed skirt are Egerton Paisley in Red combined with a vintage French quilt on the bed.

ABOVE A tranquil dining area down by the water. This is such a sheltered spot that swimming here feels like you're in a private natural swimming pool. The classic rattan outdoor furniture is from Sika Design, while the tablecloth is Kirkbean in Red (Turquoise).

RIGHT The untouched interior of the summerhouse was furnished with existing furniture. I simply gave it a coat of Benjamin Moore paint to bring it back to life.

OPPOSITE This charming shingled structure has hosted many a party. The Kennedys, when in office, would spend weekends relaxing here with their great friends the Mellons.

MANHATTAN

Anne McNally and I met through our husbands Brian and Gary, who had become friends in New York, where Brian had started the legendary restaurant Indochine with his brother. Coincidentally, Anne's father was French and owned a house in the village of Bruniquel, close to my farm in south-west France. Her two children, Jessica and James, and my three, Oscar, Otis, and Louis, have been lifelong friends.

On one visit to France, Anne stayed in my newly renovated *pigeonnier* and liked the tonal cream palette so much that she asked if I would redo her West Village townhouse. What she didn't realize was that the duck canvas I had used for my slipcovers and curtains was not only chosen for its chicness but also for its cheapness. I'd learned this trick from one of my mentors, Nico, who swapped her title from Marchioness to Mrs. She used plain canvas at her own farmhouse in Somerset, but embellished the soft furnishings with colored trims.

I admire people who trust their own taste despite changing trends, and Anne does exactly that. With her fashion background, having been an editor at *Vogue* and *Vanity Fair*, she is always ahead of the curve. Just as I expected, her New York townhouse had elegant dimensions and a good flow. However, the hallway and dining room needed a few special pieces, and on a trip to England I came across the *pièce de résistance* for this space—an 80in./2m.-round tabletop made from a single piece of marble, something I had never seen before. Of course, I was terrified that it would not arrive in New York all in one piece, but thank goodness it did. To this day, that tabletop remains one of my favorite finds of all time.

Other pieces were sourced in Los Angeles. At Lief, we found an enchanting Gustavian settee, as well as a pair of early 18th-century carved chairs along with a Biedermeier desk. For Anne's bedroom, I used duck canvas for the curtains, adding a Colefax & Fowler trim, and a couple of vintage ivory chenille bedcovers that I'd found were remade into slipcovers for the cozy reading chair and ottoman. The ceiling beams were whitewashed throughout and we restored the wide-plank wooden flooring to its original mahogany hue. My younger brother Robert project-managed the job on site—we were used to renovations in the suburban sprawl of LA, so the narrow streets of New York City were a challenge for both of us.

Once finished, the house returned to party central—Anne continues to be a fashion muse, and with her interest in the arts, fashion, and food she is a prominent figure in New York society.

PAGE 179 The restored shutters are the focal point in this room, which is home to Anne's desk. The walls are lined with built-in bookcases. The standing lamp came from Vaughan and I found the small French chair in Montauban.

OPPOSITE AND RIGHT The original hardwood floors in this room have been refinished. The generous Chelsea Textiles crewelwork curtains flank a Swedish settee and chairs found at Lief in Los Angeles. The center table was found at Talisman Antiques in Dorset, England, which has since closed— the founder Ken Bolan now has a studio in Wiltshire. A painting by Antonio Murado hangs on the wall.

I always liken decorating to cooking—one too many ingredients throws the whole taste off.

OPPOSITE AND THIS PAGE A very neutral palette was the order of the day for the master bedroom. Its simple cotton duck canvas curtains are edged with a Colefax & Fowler trim. The fireplaces throughout are original to the house.

ANOTHER COUNTRY

After successfully finishing Anne's New York brownstone, she came to stay with me in France. At the time, I was finalizing my first fabric collection, Quilt, and spending lots of time surrounded by overflowing baskets filled with strike-offs from the hand-printing factories and samples of weaves from various European and English mills. Anne has impeccable taste, so of course I welcomed her comments. In her very French, very Anne way, she rummaged through everything and remarked how well some of my designs would suit her New England farmhouse in the Litchfield Hills of Connecticut.

Most homeowners decorating a house themselves will leave the window treatments to the very end of the process, but as an interior designer I have always worked the other way round —fabrics are the starting point for me in any room. However, Anne was quite right in her intuition, and when I eventually got the chance to visit her at her farm in Connecticut, I saw immediately how my fabrics would enhance her existing décor.

Whether it's a rustic retreat or an impossibly elegant Parisian flat on the Place des Vosges, Anne knows exactly how to furnish a home. To anyone else's eyes, the farmhouse would have looked finished—this was country living at its most elegant. However, as soon as I brought out my big bag of swatches, it was very easy to place the Quilt collection, which consisted of six designs in six colorways. The patterns were so perfectly suited to the farmhouse that each one almost sailed through the air to the right room and found its own place, from Quilt Red in the kitchen to Ikat Green in the bedroom and Ikat Yellow in the sitting room.

In those days, Susan Maltby, my design lieutenant and most trusted seamstress, traveled with me constantly. The two of us soon pulled Anne's place together with new curtains, slipcovers, and pillows. The prints we selected from that first collection immediately brought the farmhouse to life. As a newcomer to the field of textile design back then, I was so lucky to have a friend like Anne who invited me to adorn her house with my new fabrics.

Now, 25 years on, after normal wear and tear, sun damage, and accident have left their mark on these same window treatments, Anne has decided to replace them with identical versions made from the same patterned fabrics from that very first collection. When she told me of her plans, I asked her, "Anne, don't you want to try something new?" To which she responded, "When you strike oil, why dig deeper?"

PAGE 185 This is one of my all-time favorite shots—a "real" still life featuring my Quilt design in Red, the first colorway of my first-ever fabric design. Anne's son (and my godson) James McNally, when looking at the proofs for this book, exclaimed "The house is still exactly the same all these years later."

RIGHT The English dining table and mismatched wooden chairs were sourced locally by Anne. The blanket thrown over the sofa was made from a favorite Raoul Textiles design.

LEFT The sitting room opens onto the living room next door. The chairs are slipcovered and drawn up around a large pouffe covered with a patchwork of Bennison fabric, which centers the room. The Roman shade is made from my Ikat design in the Yellow colorway.

OPPOSITE The living room has doors out to the covered porch beyond, from which light floods into the old farmhouse.

The use of color and how it is assembled in a room creates the picture.

ABOVE The simplicity of this bathroom is true to the period in which the house was built. The accents of wood and the color of the windows and trim are very much in keeping with the origins of the building.

RIGHT Anne's Indian bed is decorated with one of my sheers. The bedcover and hand-painted bedside table were both found on a buying trip in France. The Roman shades are made from Ikat in Green and the robe from Paisley Stripe in Red.

BRITISH ISLES

My fundamental love and yearning for the tradition that was part of my upbringing is at the heart of this collection. I was drawn to more subdued, tea-stained shades that are reminiscent of my childhood home on the west coast of Scotland.

COMING HOME

A couple of years ago, my sister and I were renovating our old family home in southwest London close to the river and the park when an opportunity arose for me to move north of the Thames. My new house was on a small gem of a street tucked in at the top of Gloucester Road, and strolling in nearby Kensington Gardens immediately transported me back to my childhood. I walked in this park with my classmates at Glendower School on our afternoon outings, and played ponies here with my best friend Cosima Vane-Tempest-Stewart. I felt as if I was coming home.

For the first few months in the house, I lived out of a suitcase. That old saying "The cobbler never has shoes"—well, that was me! But with a new fabric collection on the horizon, and a torn meniscus, there was only so long I could sit on the floor surrounded by fabric swatches and sketches. I was ready to have a sofa to sit on and a table to work from.

I've known this house for many years, as it is the home of my childhood friend Patrick, and I imagined it had been patiently waiting for me to return and shower it with love. It has beautiful Georgian reception rooms that stretch from the

street to the garden, one opening onto the next. A well-proportioned fireplace distinguishes each of these rooms and they are hung with a pair of 19th-century crystal chandeliers. Sometimes existing architectural elements can be a nuisance, but not when you're dealing with a house whose original features are all intact. All it needed was my trademark dashes of color and quirk to revive its excellent 18th-century bones.

I was lucky enough to find an old Howard sofa at my upholsterers, and asked them to reupholster it. As luck would have it, my warehouse had mistakenly sent double quantities of Otis Textiles Mohair for a project, which turned out to be very handy. Howard & Sons sofas, like AGA cookers, are quintessentially British and are becoming more difficult to come by. (They're so good, no one parts with them.) Not only did my new/old sofa anchor the room but it also became the source of inspiration for its redesign.

PAGE 194 My East Meets West collection is the backdrop to the living rooms in my 19th-century house in London. When *Milieu* magazine asked to feature the house, the heat was on to finish this room. It was nearly impossible to find a pair of bookcases to fit on both sides of the fireplace, but one of my favorite antique dealers happened to have a perfect match in the back of his van.

THIS PAGE The formal dining room, also my workroom, is anchored by a Robsjohn-Gibbings table from Orlando Harris at the Blanchard Collective. The mirror and side tables are from Julian Chichester. The lamps are both 19th-century English and the matching Oka shades trick the eye into thinking them a pair. The French chairs are covered in my Kippford Stripe and the curtain fabric is Hilltop Paisley Regal from the Jewels of the East collection.

Only in the West Country can you ramble down a muddy lane and stumble across an old barn full of antiques. It was here that I found two armchairs in need of a full overhaul. Once rescued from obscurity, I reupholstered them in brightly striped fabric from my most recent collection.

The house was the ideal place to showcase my new paisley-patterned Hilltop fabric. Over the years, I have amassed a fabulous cache of vintage textiles and one gilt and carnelian scrap proved to be the perfect remnant with which to cover the ottoman in the living room. And I sourced some great paintings from one of my favorite dealers in Tetbury.

My London storage facility is something of an Aladdin's cave. It's crammed with pieces bought for future projects, items I'm waiting to place on a job, and family hand-me-downs that will one day find a home. But even with the addition of furnishings from this private stash, there were still gaps. Luckily, my dear friends in the trade, Julian Chichester and Orlando Harris, came to the rescue with a vanload of mirrors, lamps, and other bits and pieces that add the perfect finishing touches.

In this London townhouse, merging the classic proportions of a Georgian house with fresh, vital color in the shape of contemporary art, textiles, and furnishings was such a thrill. At first, I wasn't sure how to decorate around the late 18th-century chandeliers that were already in situ. But once I got going, the rooms spoke to me, as they always do, and somehow, magically, I made them work. Now the chandeliers play a starring role, and I can't even imagine not having them there.

LEFT The ceramic 1950s vase was sourced at Greenway Antiques, Witney, while the plates are Spanish, circa 1920, and were found at Gallery B.R in Tetbury.

OPPOSITE Looking through the two reception rooms on the raised ground floor. The late 18th-century chandeliers came from Kensington Church Street and the painting is by Angela Francis. Samples of tiles and my latest weaves are fanned out on the table.

ABOVE At the beginning of my career, I gave a revamp to Steve Martin's modern house in Santa Barbara. His art was large-scale and contemporary and I learned then to take my lead from the colours in the paintings, something I continue to do today. The painting here is by Claudia Valsells from Gallery B.R in Tetbury, England.

RIGHT My Howard sofa is upholstered in Otis Textiles Mohair in Fig, while the hand-dyed pillow covers are by Kirsten Hecktermann. On the wall are Tonga baskets from Zambia. The ottoman is covered in an antique textile that I found at The Decorative Antiques and Textiles Fair in Battersea.

LEFT AND ABOVE In the bedroom, the painting between the windows is by Lydia Corbett, a muse of Picasso's who is still painting and showing at the Fosse Gallery in Stow-on-the-Wold. The crewelwork curtain fabric came from Louisa Maybury Textiles in Woodstock, Oxfordshire, while the bedspread is vintage Chelsea Textiles. Two paintings by Maria Yelletisch found at Gallery B.R in Tetbury hang on the wall opposite the windows.

ABOVE The basement, once a rabbit warren of small rooms, is now open plan and stretches the length of the house. With its low ceilings, keeping it simple and free of window treatments to ensure maximum light was key. The painting is by Max Cobalto from Gallery B.R in Tetbury.

RIGHT The 25-year-old Bulthaup kitchen still stands the test of time, only needing some simple accessories and a few pieces of art to refresh and update the space. The vintage table is by Patrick Moore and the painting just in view on the wall is by Joanna Carrington.

PAGES 206–207 This little nook was originally a passage to an exterior staircase leading to the garden, then a study, and is now a guest room. The bedcover is my own Sultan Suzani dressed with an abundance of velvet pillows.

A TALE OF TWO CITIES

aving just completed his house in the Hollywood Hills, I received a call from my client asking if I'd not only design the interiors for his newly acquired farmhouse in the Cotswolds, but also oversee the entire renovation. This sort of job is my forte—I always love a big project where I can get to grips with the interior architecture and garden design. In addition, one thing that gets my heart racing is any mention of the Cotswolds, to me the most enchanting of English landscapes. My client is one of the UK's most talented actors and working with him on his LA home had been a joy, so obviously my answer was yes.

I was yearning for an excuse to come home for a while, and this job gave me the perfect opportunity. Even better, this new country place came with a fun provenance. The farmhouse was previously the home of Sir Mark Palmer, hippie baronet and former page to his godmother Queen Elizabeth II, and his wife, the astrologer Catherine Tennant. Everyone I'd ever known had a story about it during its hedonistic heyday. When I told Lady Jane Churchill that I was doing the house, she immediately shared an anecdote, "Oh, my dear, when I went to stay and said I had to have a bath, I was handed a tennis ball—that was the bath plug!"

Charming though it was, the house needed more than just new curtains and throw pillows. But the prospect of a full-scale restoration delights me. I knew I wanted to retain the original footprint of the house while preserving and enhancing its many quirks and charms. This was a listed building of historic importance and work on the roof had to be delayed for months while the resident bats were rehoused. Luckily, I found an architect and a local contractor who were well versed in dealing with properties of this type. We wanted to preserve the patina of the centuries and stay true to the spirit of the house and the people who had lived there before.

PAGE 209 The master bedroom is wallpapered in my Marrakech Natural in Teal, accompanied by a French armchair upholstered in Pampas Teal by Andrew Martin. The armoire is from Lorfords in Tetbury, while the Kente cloth was made by the Ashanti tribe in Ghana. My love for Ghanaian fabrics began in the early 1980s, when making a documentary on new religions.

LEFT AND RIGHT This room was finished apart from the painting over the fireplace, which was found at The Decorative Antiques and Textiles Fair in Battersea. The lampshades are Vaughan, and the smaller artworks came from Oka. Bouclé from C&C Milano and velvet by Lewis & Wood bring luxurious texture to the upholstery. The tables are from Macintosh Antiques in Sherborne, Dorset.

For inspiration, I turned to Jasper Conran's Instagram account for images of his ravishing 17th-century Dorset retreat. We also visited my schoolfriend Rosie Pearson's home at Asthall Manor, the former abode of the Mitford sisters. Rosie's gardens, designed by mutual friends Isabel and Julian Bannerman, are the exquisite backdrop for her *On Form* sculpture exhibition every other summer.

When it was time to furnish the house, I scoured the surrounding countryside for unique pieces. For me, antiquing, or sourcing, is all about the thrill of the hunt, and the random element of luck cannot be underestimated. I made a couple of lucky strikes whizzing around Pimlico Road and at my favorite hunting ground, The Decorative Antiques and Textiles Fair in Battersea, for pieces that had eluded me. Finding that last element that finishes a room often feels like a miracle and still surprises me sometimes.

Since buying and renovating my house in Ojai (see pages 112–121), this is the first house that has really got under my skin. If it ever comes up for sale, I've told my client that I've got first dibs on it.

LEFT The centerpiece of the formal sitting room is a wall hanging found at the Joss Graham Gallery in London. The ottoman is upholstered in Kintbury Stripe from the Guy Goodfellow Collection and the curtains were made from panels found at Louisa Maybury Textiles in Woodstock, Oxfordshire. The club fender came from Jamb and the original Chesterfield from Patricia Harvey Antiques. It is flanked by a pair of standing lamps from Macintosh Antiques, where I also sourced the spectacular gilt overmantel mirror. The chandelier was carefully carried all the way back from France in hand luggage.

ABOVE The dining room, which also serves as a library, has a Jacobean gateleg table from John Howard in Woodstock, Oxfordshire. The wood carvings on the wall came from Maison & Objet in Paris.

RIGHT Wing chairs upholstered in blue corduroy from Tissus d'Hélène present a bold contrast to the red walls. The curtain fabric is Hilltop Paisley Regal from my *Jewels of the East* collection. Over the fireplace hangs a textile artwork by Marcia Bennett-Male, which I found at the *On Form* sculpture show at Asthall Manor.

LEFT The dining table was bought from the Blanchard Collective in Marlborough, England, while the chairs are from Howe London. Curtains in my Bukhara Suzani fabric bring a hint of color and pattern.

RIGHT Cosmo Fry's elegant plate rack takes center stage in the kitchen.

BELOW As a throwback to the bohemian tastes of the former owners Sir Mark Palmer and Catherine Tennant, we repainted the utility room and laundry woodwork in their original yellow. I believe in keeping the integrity of a building wherever possible.

OPPOSITE The back staircase, which leads up from the dining room, has a classic striped runner from Roger Oates Design. The paintings above the fireplace are by Claude Palmier.

RIGHT Leaves Red from my wallpaper collection continues all the way up the stairs to the landing, which is lined with a series of vintage runners that came from Albi, France. The curtains were made from two bedspreads that I found at Louisa Maybury Textiles in Woodstock, Oxfordshire. Vaughan's Pumpkin Globe Lantern hangs from the ceiling while the mirror just glimpsed at the end of the hallway is 18th-century French.

LEFT A hand-carved bed by Elliott & Co is teamed with an Indian wall hanging. The flatweave underfoot was made by the Swedish brand Vandra Rugs. A small chair covered in Otis Textiles' Kid Mohair Oyster completes the scheme.

ABOVE My trademark painted bathtub is seen here in Farrow & Ball's Rectory Red. The curtain fabric is my Sheer Confetti Red. All the bathroom fixtures are from C.P. Hart.

OPPOSITE This room happens to have two of my favorites from my second fabric collection, Toile and Ikat Check, both in Red. The pillows and bedcover are from Louisa Maybury Textiles and the lamps were made by the ceramicist Miranda Berrow.

ABOVE Curtains should never be more than twice the width of the window, in my opinion. These pinch-pleat drapes were sewn onto the iron rings by hand.

RIGHT This French chair from Emma Lascelles Antiques in Tetbury is upholstered in my Hand Stitched fabric. The pastel artwork below the window came from John Howard in Woodstock.

OPPOSITE This one-time outhouse is now a bedroom with a headboard and bedskirt in my Hand Stitched Multi. The two bedside lamps came from Greenway Antiques in Witney, while the bolster was made from a scarf found at Louise Maybury Textiles in Woodstock, Oxfordshire.

BELOW One of the renovated bathrooms features my Casablanca wallpaper with Roman shades in Sheer Confetti Snow.

RIGHT The hand-sewn Indian Mirror fabric used for the curtains in this bedroom is a new addition to my textile line. It was inspired by a bedspread that once belonged to Nico, Marchioness of Londonderry, my best friend Cosima's mother and my mentor.

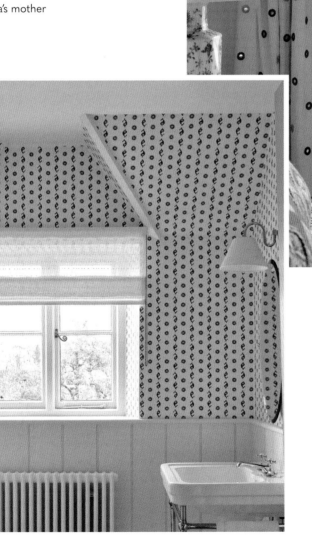

When it comes to accessorizing, I hunt out pieces of interesting fabric that can be turned into lampshades or throw pillows.

SUMMER IN FRANCE

When I was raising my three boys, my family and I divided our time between Southern California and south-west France. The undulating countryside and Tuscan-style architecture of the Languedoc region inspired this collection.

A PLACE IN THE SUN

My charming Texan clients, who have roots in both England and France, are the current chatelains of this picturesque compound on the Normandy coast, which has been in their family for the past 150 years. Over time, I have had the pleasure of helping them restore the three houses on the property to accommodate their ever-growing family and many friends.

My clients' initial enthusiasm for the project of renovating this long-time family holiday home was dampened by the difficulties of finding a local architect and designer. However, as chance would have it, they saw an *Elle Decor* piece on my house in France and immediately got in touch with me, an Englishwoman from Los Angeles who had successfully renovated her own home in France and spoke some French.

When they first took on the property, the three buildings, arranged around a garden and close to the sea, needed a refresh. The lack of bathrooms was a major concern—the buildings had few of the usual American comforts and needed updating so the family and their visitors could enjoy the house all year round.

My clients flirted with the idea of tearing down one of the three existing houses due to the fact that it was almost at the point of no return, but I begged them to leave it standing—as I always say, never do anything that you might one day regret. Instead, I advised that we start by focusing on the principal house and the main guest house, both of which were habitable. Luckily, my powers of persuasion worked and they asked me to redesign the interiors, manage the renovation, and decorate the restored buildings. As it happens, some years later, after I'd finished these two buildings, I was asked to return to renovate the forgotten *maison d'amis*.

Luckily for me, the construction team I had been working with in London were French and came to France to work with me on the renovation. The contractor Jean's family are from Bordeaux, and he happens to work between the UK and France.

This was a top-to-toe refurbishment, and the budget was primarily allocated to gutting the properties, replumbing and rewiring, restoring the windows and doors, and replacing two staircases, as well as adding those much-needed additional bathrooms.

I was conscious that, for the most part, this was a summer house and the lion's share of the budget needed to go into the guts of the building rather than the decoration. My UK workshop made all the curtains and slipcovers and updated the existing soft furnishings, and I enjoyed sourcing the rest of the contents at the local dealers close to my home in southern France. I persuaded my charming local taxi driver to rent a van and drive it all the way to Normandy, stuffed to the gills with pottery and rugs plus the perfect kitchen island, which I'd spotted in my local florist in Montauban.

My clients were as pleased with the results as I was proud that I'd delivered the house in less than a year. Every summer, I receive photos of their kids and grandkids at the family's summer home and a note thanking me for restoring their ancestral beach house for them and future generations.

PAGE 229 The patchwork bedcover, which manages to get into every house I do, was made up from my first fabric collection, Quilt, which was inspired by an 18th-century quilt. The headboard and curtains are in my Lola in Green.

PAGES 230–231 In the main guest house, an industrial metal staircase replaced the existing wooden one, which had begun to rot. I oriented the new staircase the other way around so that you wouldn't tumble into it when entering the front door. The dining table and chairs are from Sika-Design. Curtains in my Safi Suzani complement various colorful pillows.

LEFT The simple rustic kitchen retained its original flooring and tile, with the addition of storage baskets and a curtain made from my Moroccan Stripe.

RIGHT I found this display table in Zeste, my local flower shop in Montauban, and snapped it up to use as the kitchen island. Various plates and glasses were sourced from the local IKEA and the light fixtures are by Original BTC.

OPPOSITE In this very narrow bedroom, the only way to fit in two beds was to place them end to end. This configuration is perfect for a children's room, as each of the two occupants has their own nook for books and other small objects. The bedcovers are made from Hand Stitched in Red and the pillow fabric is Toile in Teal. The framed original Tintin book cover came from a Paris flea market.

RIGHT A selection of brightly colored African baskets that I sourced from the Saturday morning market in Montauban, near Toulouse.

BELOW An artwork by Rose Electra Harris and shades in Greta Reverse Red bring vibrant color to the simple wood-paneled bathroom. The washstand is from Duravit and the chair already belonged to the clients.

ABOVE AND LEFT The main house has the typical steep hipped roofs and arched dormer windows of the region and overlooks the vast white beach with the Atlantic Ocean beyond.

OPPOSITE Rattan garden chairs from Sika-Design surround a table found at the flea market in Albi and create an inviting spot for breakfast or lunch.

THE FRENCH CONNECTION

My friendship with Anne Halsey dates back to a chance meeting in a London pizzeria sometime in the 1980s. As luck would have it, we both started married life on the same street in Santa Monica, California, and when Amanda Pays and I turned Gary's and my then editing suite into a decorative accessories shop, Anne ran it for us, taking to retail like a duck to water. When she moved back to London some years later, at the time when my textile career had just taken off, she and I opened a showroom in London that represented not only my lines but also those of many other Californian designers.

Anne and her family were frequent houseguests at La Castellane, my house in France (see pages 252–267). On one such trip, she came along with me to look at a house on behalf of a mutual friend who was hunting for her very own French getaway. It was a dull February day and the two of us drove along a bumpy dirt track to find ourselves at a cluster of several 17th-century stone buildings. The little hamlet consisted of a main house and a number of outbuildings, including a *pigeonnier*, plus a swimming pool, and an established garden. Some of the other buildings were almost ruins, but their original masonry had been salvaged and repurposed into charming stone walls. At the time, Anne had absolutely no interest in buying a house in the area—for one thing, she very much enjoyed staying with me. But with a push from her husband, and the reassurance that I could have them moved in by the summer, they took the plunge and bought this magical hamlet.

As a veteran of these French country houses, I have grown more practical with each renovation. When visiting a charming old stone property, I now ignore its picturesque good looks and make a beeline for the attics to inspect the eaves, because replacing roofs and chimneys can be extremely expensive, while water damage often causes wiring and floorboard issues. However, as luck would have it, these charming buildings had been surprisingly well

239

PAGES 238 AND 239 Once a kitchen, this room was converted to a bathroom. Eager not to lose the authenticity of the space, a modern basin was added to the old sink (page 238). Looking down on the property from the back garden of the main house. The *pigeonnier* is something of a local landmark (page 239).

LEFT The living room of the house with the original fireplace, also built of the local limestone. Parts of the hamlet are hundreds of years old and the cupboard doors date back to when the house was built.

maintained with just minor cosmetic defects. However, although some of the buildings had already been restored, there was still much work to be done.

The bones of the main house were good but the layout wasn't ideal, so I reconfigured the interior, enlarging the existing bedrooms and adding bathrooms while relocating the kitchen to a roomier situation in an adjacent barn. A relatively recently converted art studio on the upper floor of the main residence was divided up into a couple of bathrooms. Wherever possible, I kept the original elements: all the fireplaces were intact, and there were many other architectural features, such as the stone sinks.

The construction work was finished in a few months, leaving me plenty of time to furnish the interiors. Here, I used fabrics from every one of my collections to add comfort and color to the charming rustic rooms. It was wonderful to see this beautiful old French house come to life for the Halseys, and for me too, especially since it meant having my childhood friend so close to me in France.

OPPOSITE ABOVE Large glass double doors were added to the new kitchen and lead out onto a terrace that's often used for breakfast and lunch.

OPPOSITE BELOW A practical butler's pantry-cum-bar connects the new kitchen with the dining room (not shown).

THIS PAGE A former barn was converted into a bright and airy kitchen. Being a Cordon Bleu-trained cook, Anne had much to say about what went where and the layout of the room.

ABOVE AND LEFT In the guest bedroom, we hid the toilet in a cupboard that looks as if it's been there forever. All the soft furnishings here are in my Toile print in Red, and a Vaughan glass lamp and an antique quilt on the bed add to the timeless charm of the room.

OPPOSITE What the house most lacked was bathrooms, but bringing a 200-year-old house up to modern standards is not easy. Chasing wires into either stone or mud walls and inserting waste pipes for lavatories, bathtubs, and basins was challenging. In this guest room, I sat the bathtub on a platform and kept it in the room—there's nothing worse than small poky bathrooms.

PAGES 246–247 With its high ceilings, the main bedroom has wonderful proportions. The curtains are in Raoul Textiles' Mahatma design with my Small Check on the bed tester. Anne and I represented Raoul in our London showroom, along with other Californian fabric lines.

ABOVE An outdoor sitting area faces west, making it a delightful place for early evening rendezvous while the sun goes down. In the background is the old bakery, now used for storage and summer entertaining but no longer to make fresh bread, alas.

RIGHT The door seen on page 238 leads out onto this pretty rose-draped terrace. Like me, Anne loves entertaining friends and family, so many of the old barns and outbuildings have been converted into pretty guest rooms where everyone can enjoy a sense of privacy.

OPPOSITE When Anne found the property, some of the original buildings were in complete disrepair and some had already been demolished. Luckily, the stone was repurposed for building walls and flower beds. This sheltered courtyard beneath a wisteria vine is the perfect lunch spot, tucked away in a corner of the garden.

SUR LA PLAGE

The inspiration for this collection came from the eastern coastline of the US, from Cape Cod to Palm Beach. The simple yet charming designs are ideal for a multitude of climates, from the Caribbean to the Scandinavian archipelago.

LES ENFANTS DU PARADIS

n the early years of our marriage, Gary and I had a production company producing music videos for Paul Simon, The Bangles, and George Harrison, to name but a few. When we flew over to shoot a video in London, I saw a chance for us to go on a much-needed French honeymoon.

After winding our way down through France, we ended up in the Tarn. Gary's pal Brian McNally had suggested that if we found ourselves that far south, we should scour this picture-postcard region for a property, and we did. I fell in love with the very first house we saw. It was February and there wasn't a sunflower in sight—just derelict stone buildings, broken tractors, and old farm junk. Within days the paperwork was completed.

Once back in Los Angeles, I started to regret our hasty decision to become absentee owners of a French ruin 5,000 miles away. Fortunately, our dear friends Berry Berenson and Tony Perkins were adamant that I maintain a tangible link to my own history and geography and extinguished every doubt I had about the purchase.

Our new/old house had been built in 1750 and needed new everything—electrical wiring, plumbing, and roofs. The main residence had only two bedrooms and a living room, plus attic. I converted a cow barn into a kitchen and living area, added some French doors and a window or two, and renovated the *pigeonnier* into a guest house.

Over time, I added a pool and refurbished the stables. I planted a kitchen garden and made valiant attempts at coaxing the vineyard into viability. I brought in goats for milk and chickens for eggs and Arab mares for a horse-breeding sideline, all to defray expenses incurred in my French folly. Each gambit added to the vitality of the compound, and some almost broke even. It took 20 years to get the house to where it is today: a beautifully restored working farm that comfortably sleeps 16 people.

I remain steadfast in my commitment to La Castellane and to France. My second son, Otis, was married here. His daughter, my first grandchild, will soon spend her first summer here. Gratefully, my family will continue to gather at La Castellane for a great many years to come.

PAGE 252 When I turned down a remote dirt road one day in February, who knew that when I returned that summer I was to be surrounded by sunflowers—my very own sunflowers!

PAGES 254–255 The one-time cow byre-turned-family room/kitchen is the hub of the house. I installed the fireplace on top of the manger, which runs the length of the room. The collection of local jugs were the result of a challenge I had with Christopher Howe one summer: Whoever found the smallest jug got to keep the collection that we had put together.

LEFT For the first few years we used the original kitchen, but this space was crying out to be used on a daily basis. The terracotta squares were locally sourced in Montauban, while the wall tiles came from Provence. The AGA sits majestically at one end of the room. French doors open onto the outdoor dining room (previously used for machinery storage) and a door leads into what was the wine cellar but has now become our prep kitchen.

ABOVE The house is full of art and personal pieces like this framed artwork, a gift from my dear friend Robin Birley whose love of dogs is ever apparent.

ABOVE A vignette from the hallway. The curtains are in my Safi Suzani design in the Autumn colorway while the candle sconce was a birthday present from Christopher Howe. The baseball oil painting is by Steven Skollar.

RIGHT On the ground floor, my library is home to an eclectic collection of family photographs, personal memorabilia, and hand-me-down furniture. The coffee table is by Roger Capron, a 20th-century ceramicist from Vallauris.

OPPOSITE This room was turned back to its original form. There had been a makeshift bathroom at the far end and the door was repurposed here when the new doorway was installed. One of my many quilts covers the bed—I change them according to the season. The painting was a gift from Barry Dixon and I had the chair slipcovered in a chenille bedcover.

ABOVE I turned a bedroom into an oversize bathroom hung with art by my kids and close friends, much of it created for my 40th birthday. This armchair is the most used chair in the house.

LEFT My Bouquet fabric in Coral Blue covers the headboard and works perfectly with the 1950s ceramic lamp. I always like to have a stack of books by the bed—compiling libraries for clients is one of my favorite pastimes. The photograph is by Thurston Hopkins and came from the Peter Fetterman Gallery in Los Angeles.

ABOVE AND RIGHT The Ralph Lauren wicker beds were bought at a yard sale in Montecito and were shipped over in the early days along with our old Audi, which I stuffed full of bedding, crockery, pots and pans, and all the other essentials for an instant kitchen. The head- and footboards are covered in slipcovers made from my Toile in Indigo and the duvet covers are Diamond Batik in Indigo. The bed pillows came from John Robshaw, while the framed Wegman poster was a gift to Gary from the artist.

LEFT What was once the farm office is now a guest bedroom. I left the original hardwood floors as they were. The only drawback of this room is that it opens beneath to the Dutch barn—not great if you're an early nighter, as the dinners below can go into the small hours. The fabric used throughout is Lilac Red from my Sur La Plage collection. All the bathroom sinks, toilets, and bidets throughout the house came from Duravit's 1930s collection.

ABOVE One of my three black Arabs, Nazullah. I'm always up for an early morning ride.

LEFT, ABOVE LEFT, AND OPPOSITE The property, with its 50 acres, has many places to dine throughout the day. The Dutch barn opposite was once used for milking the cows—the farmer we bought from bred Blonde d'Aquitaine cattle, local to this area of France. The majestic oak tree in the garden overlooks the Tescou valley and our sunflower fields on one side, and on the other has a view of the farmhouse. This is our favorite lunch spot (above left).

PICTURE CREDITS

Key: Ph = photographer; a = above; b = below; l = left; c = centre; r = right.

Front cover Ph Trevor Tondro; back cover portrait Ph Deborah Anderson. The front endpapers feature personal photographs, except for the following: top row, left to right: portrait Ph Joanna Johnston; fireplace Ph Tim Beddow; wedding Ph Lucy Birkhead. Middle row, left to right: portrait with horse Ph Mikkel Vang; bench with cushion Ph Miguel Flores-Vianna; family portrait Ph Dewey Nicks. Bottom row, left to right: bed and portrait Ph Tim Beddow. The back endpapers feature personal photographs, except for the following: top row left to right: hallway Ph Francois Halard; family portrait Ph Alexandre Bailhache; wedding party Ph Lucy Birkhead. Middle row, left to right: portrait Ph Thibault Jeanson; photograph of Otis, Courtney, and Georgina Ph Natasha Halimi. Bottom row left to right: fabric rolls Ph John Hugstad; bedroom, gingham armchair, and market Ph Tim Beddow. Page 1 Ph Trevor Tondro; 2 Ph James Merrell; 3 Ph John Hugstad; 4 Ph James Merrell; 6 Ph Deborah Anderson; 8 Nicolette, the Marchioness of Londonderry; 9 a & bl Ph Tim Beddow; 9 br Ph Dewey Nicks/House & Garden US; 10-11 artwork by Lucilla Caine; 12-15 Ph Tim Beddow; 16-17 fabrics by Kathryn M. Ireland; 17-25 Ph Trevor Tondro; 26 Ph Tim Beddow; 27 Ph Trevor Tondro; 28-29 Ph Tim Beddow; 30-32 Ph Trevor Tondro; 33 a Ph Sue Huddleston; 33 b Ph Trevor Tondro; 34-35 Ph Trevor Tondro; 36 Ph Trevor Tondro; 37-39 Ph Tim Beddow; 40-45 Ph Trevor Tondro; 46-47 Ph Tim Beddow; 48-49 Ph Trevor Tondro; 50-51 fabrics by Kathryn M. Ireland; 52-59 Ph Tim Beddow; 60-66 l Ph Richard Powers; 66-67 Ph Trevor Tondro; 68-69 Ph Richard Powers; 70-71 Ph Trevor Tondro; 72-73 Ph Richard Powers; 74 Ph Trevor Tondro; 75 Ph Richard Powers; 76-79 Ph Tim Beddow; 80-81 Ph Andreas Von Einsiedel; 82-87 Ph Tim Beddow; 88-95 Ph Tess Albrecht; 96-109 Ph Vicky Pearson; 110-111 fabrics by Kathryn M. Ireland; 112 Ph Thibault Jeanson/Vogue Living; 113 Ph Tim Beddow; 114-119 Ph Vicky Pearson; 120-121 Ph Dewey Nicks; 122-131 Ph Tim Beddow; 132-143 Ph Isabel Parra; 144-163 Ph Tim Beddow; 164-165 fabrics by Kathryn M. Ireland; 166 Ph Trel Brock; 167-171 Ph James Merrell; 172 Ph Trel Brock; 173-177 Ph James Merrell; 178-191 Ph Tim Beddow; 192-193 fabrics by Kathryn M. Ireland; 194-207 Ph James Merrell; 208-225 Ph James Merrell; 226-227 fabrics by Kathryn M. Ireland; 228-237 Ph Tim Beddow; 238-249 Ph Tim Beddow; 250-251 fabrics by Kathryn M. Ireland; 252-265 Ph Tim Beddow; 266 al Ph Tim Hardy; ar Ph Mikkel Vang; bl Ph Tim Beddow; 267 Ph Tim Beddow; 269 Ph James Merrell.

Kathryn's website can be found at www.kathrynireland.com and her Instagram account is @kathrynmireland.

INDEX

ACKNOWLEDGEMENTS

Thank you to my clients and industry friends who provide inspiration and projects to work on, in particular Lady Annabel Goldsmith, who gave me a bedroom in her house to decorate with my first textile collection. Thank you for all the hard work everyone has put into producing this book and for believing in me. Thanks to my clients Julie and Stephen Block, Chiwetel Ejiofor, Anne Halsey, Anne and David Heaney, Victoria Jackson and Bill Guthy, Bridget and Bill Koch, Anne McNally, Pat and Candace Malloy, Steve Martin, Patrick Moores, Nancy and Bruce Newberg, Mark Robertson, Andy Sabin, and Kari Lynn Sabin, to name but a few.

I am so grateful to my showrooms over the years; in particular John Rosselli, Grizzel & Mann, James Showroom, Charles Spada, and Tissus d'Hélène—a constant in my life. Thank you to my PRs, Josh Fearnley and Matt Walker of Period Media, who have been with me since *Million Dollar Decorators* Season 1.

Many thanks to all the fabulous photographers that have contributed to this book, especially Tim Beddow, who has documented my work from the beginning, Trevor Tondro and James Merrell, who photographed several of the most recent houses in this book, and Dewey Nicks, who took two of my favourite photos of me! Thanks too to David Murphy, who is always at the end of the phone to answer questions and advise on photographers.

Thank you to the magazine editors who commissioned stories on some of these houses and others for featuring my fabrics in their pages, in particular Margaret Russell and Whitney Robinson at *Elle Decor*, Hamish Bowles and Elise Taylor at *Vogue*, Pam Pierce at *Milieu*, Sophie Donelson and Jo Saltz at *House Beautiful*, Carolyn Englefield, Clint Smith, and Dara Caponigro at *Veranda*, Nancy Novograd at *House & Garden* US and *Travel & Leisure*, Sue Crewe and Hatta Byng at *House & Garden* UK, Lucy Searle at *Homes & Gardens*, and the late Min Hogg and Rupert Thomas at *The World of Interiors*.

Special thanks go to Anne Halsey, Kate Massa, Lucilla Caine, and Gloria Ortiz, who have stood by me and managed my madness, and to Daniel Constable at United Talent Agency for being my sounding board. Also to Michael de Leone, Lorena Medrano and Alexandra Rougeau on the textile side of life, plus both teams at Advanced Graphics and Custom Craft. And to Adam Clarke and D.A. Cooke and Jean Rocha. I am so grateful to Mel Bordeaux for helping me with the text and remembering the last 30-odd years, and to Madge Baird for the six books that precede this one. Thank you Rachel Ashwell for introducing me to my current publishers CICO Books, and to Annabel Morgan and Leslie Harrington for being so patient and helpful with the arduous task of editing 30 years of photos.

Thank you to my sister Mary Jane Russell and brother Robert Ireland for being part of my team, and my brother Allister for his years of work on Le Castellane. And to my boys, Oscar, Otis, and Louis Weis, who have put up with endless photo shoots since they were little. Also to Courtney Wartman Weis and Kate Friedman, the daughters I was waiting for. And, of course, Georgina Alice, our latest addition.

And, lastly, thank you Gary Weis who, even though we lived in California, was up for buying a farm in France. The beginning of my Life in Design.

Kathryn